P9-EEM-842

BUT I LIKE IT

B
I
LIKE
iT
FANTAGRA

- Joe Sacco -

Joe Sacco

...and here's Matthew Moshkittens explaining how he's set himself apart from the grunge herd...

ARGYARGPHX...

OKS

Special thanks to Alain David, Christof Ellinghaus, Amalie Roberts, Chris Slusarenko, and Steve Turnidge

OTHER BOOKS BY JOE SACCO:

Published by Fantagraphics Books
Palestine
Safe Area Gorazde
Notes from a Defeatist

Published by Drawn and Quarterly
The Fixer
War's End

PUBLISHED BY
Fantagraphics Books, Inc.
7563 Lake City Way NE
Seattle WA 98115

Written and drawn by Joe Sacco
Edited by Kim Thompson
Designed by Adam Grano
Promotion by Eric Reynolds
Scanning and Production by Paul Baresh
Published by Gary Groth and Kim Thompson

Distributed in the U.S. by W.W. Norton and Company, Inc. (212-354-5500)
Distributed in Canada by Raincoast Books (800-663-5714)

Visit the Fantagraphics website at www.fantagraphics.com

ISBN-13: 978-1-56097-729-2
ISBN-10: 1-56097-729-9

First printing: April, 2006

Printed in Singapore

Record cover for the notoriously named German band, the Speed Niggs, or a veiled argument for gentrification? You decide.

667
J. SACCO 5-91

Portrait of the Young Man as a Young Man

by Joe Sacco ©1995

Ten years have passed and it's time to take stock... He's watched his entire world being co-opted, boiled down to its marketable essence, and sold right back to him...

He tells himself a lifestyle like his own cannot be easily replicated... Given his nurturing parents and middle-class background, it's taken a tremendous effort to get where he is today — malnourished, living on someone else's couch, and with the nipple-ring-of-the-month club threatening to hand his account over to a collection agency...

HUH?

YOU SAY SOMETHIN'?

BEEPA BEEPA BEEPA BEEPA

But something's not the same, he's not sure what... He's restless. Entertainment isn't enough. He demands to go home with a bloody nose...

Meanwhile, the spokespersons for his generation, who've just gone multi-platinum, reassure him it's just as bad at the top...

I'M STILL FULL OF ANGST AND SELF LOATHING.

YEAH. ALL THIS MONEY SUCKS

The years are slipping by. Perhaps he should ask himself some new questions, but it's only the same one that comes to mind...
AM... AM I STILL ON THE GUEST LIST?

From Spin magazine's tenth-anniversary-of-something-or-other issue.

CONTENTS

The hype engine has gone into overdrive! A dizzying plethora of local 'zines are piling us high with redundant stories of Portland bands gone big! The Spinanes this! Pond that! How much more do we need to hear about...

ROCKIN' ROSE CITY

by Joe Sacco ©1994

If all the ballyhoo is to be believed, Portland's "nationally recognized" club scene is the focal point of some sort of dazzling youth Renaissance...

HERE WE HAVE THE TWO MAIN SPECIES OF THIS SO-CALLED MOVEMENT...
WHAZAT?
I DUNNO... HOW ARE YOU GETTING HOME?
FIXTURE SATYRICONUS
UNDERAGE ERECTUS

Armed with posters and a staple-gun, another youth announces his band's entry into the "alternative music" sweepstakes...

CLAK CLAK
WAIT TILL JONATHAN* HEARS 'BOUT US!

*JONATHAN: (1) A COMMON FIRST NAME FOR A BOY; (2) A SEMI-MYTHICAL "GRUNGE" MOGUL PERSONALLY RESPONSIBLE FOR THE COLLAPSE OF WESTERN CIVILIZATION.

Meanwhile, in a SE bedroom, a Kurt Cobain-wannabe practises for his day on MTV...

WELL, I DON'T WANT YER CORPORATE AWARD!
Y'HEARD RIGHT... I DON'T WANT IT!

The city is crawling with such hopefuls, each under the delusion that pretty soon the whole world will be banging on their door for crucial personal insights...

MY MAIN INFLUENCES ARE SONIC YOUTH AND PAVEMENT.
SMELT

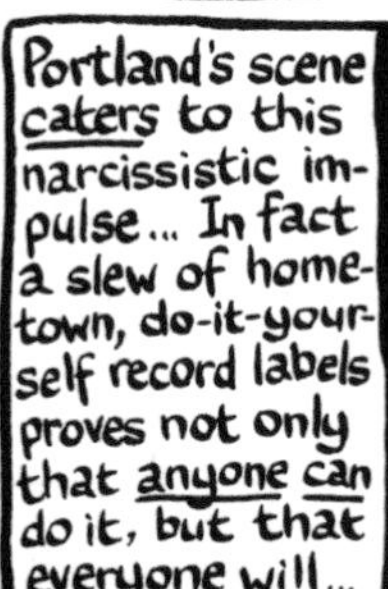

Portland's scene caters to this narcissistic impulse... In fact a slew of hometown, do-it-yourself record labels proves not only that anyone can do it, but that everyone will...

HAVE YOU HEARD MY SEVEN-INCH?
MOM!
Mrs. Sacco sings PEARL JAM
COURTNEY LOVE ANECDOTES
FOR GOD'S SAKE NOT YOU!

AH, WHAT'S THE USE? IT'LL BE THE SAME SO LONG AS ANY OL' BOZO WHO FEEDSBACK A GUITAR GARNERS MORE ACCOLADES THAN... THAN A SENSITIVE INDIVIDUAL LIKE MYSELF, WHO'S STRUGGLED YEARS IN OBSCURITY TO DEVELOP A TALENT OF AN UNDOUBTEDLY SINGULAR NATURE!!

MORE NOISE, LESS RING

I DON'T CARE... LET 'EM "MAKE MUSIC"... I'LL PRODUCE MY MASTERPIECES REGARDLESS!

And so we leave our hero, swallowing his bitterness and pressing on...

FORGET IT! I DON'T WANT YER PULITZER!
J. SACCO 1-94

From Willamette Week. "Fixture Satyriconus" refers to the patrons of the Satyricon, one of those small, dank rock clubs that seemed to have been around forever. It's no longer around.

BUSMAN'S HOLIDAY: SACCO'S ROCK AND BLUES COMICS 1988-2005

FOREWORD BY GERRY MOHR

I'VE KNOWN JOE SACCO SINCE THE MID-'70s, and one of the more remarkable things I've noticed about this very remarkable man is that in the three decades of our acquaintance I have never once known him to break wind.

I mention this fact to establish that the man is, from the very fundament of his being, a titan of restraint and self-discipline. For me, the kind of iron will his work requires — the long hours at the drawing board, every manifestation of genius arising only as its creator sits utterly, hideously alone — is no less uncanny than whatever superhuman rigor he has employed sparing his friends and enemies alike, for nearly a third of a century, any evidence that he in fact has a digestive system.

One wonders what else has been sacrificed to the demands of his art. The reader's eye dashes across the page, ignorant of the possibility that what's being absorbed in seconds owes its existence to days or even weeks of agony. After all, the comics form as we know it today doesn't necessarily, nor in every manifestation, evince belabored and demanding effort as indispensable to its creation. There are exceptions, but it can't be disputed that while much of the graphic art in comics is perhaps deceptively simple, a great deal of it is in fact exactly as simple to produce as it appears to be. Besides, for all we know, modern machinery exists that can reduce the labor of the comics artist to mere button-pushing, as it has done for so many of our Arts.

Sacco, however, prefers to pursue his calling exactly as did his elders, never once using automated cross-hatching software, never once sending his pencils to

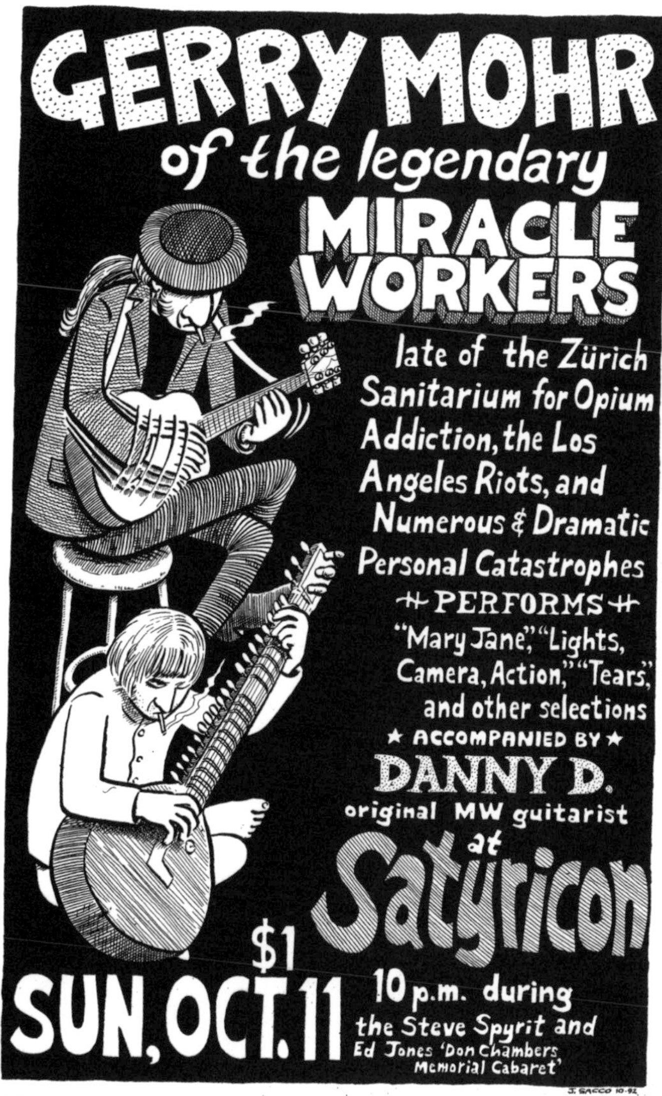

Self-explanatory flyer for Gerry Mohr's Portland "comeback."
See "The Top," pp. 59 and 60.

be sharpened in China.

Because of this it must be said it's remarkable that Sacco's managed to have such a full and varied life beyond the drawing-table. For given the obvious labor-intensiveness of his art, and its prodigious volume, one might assume that he has sustained this torrent of pages only by having foregone much of the outer life that to such an industrious worker must seem only distraction. If one decides on a path to greatness requiring, as has Sacco's, a level of time-consuming intricacy bordering on the supernatural, it would seem to follow that like cannons jettisoned from a speeding frigate, so would much of weighty random reality be of necessity tossed overboard in the quest to achieve.

But Sacco's reputation, as we now have come to understand it, is not that of the socially stunted shut-in cartoonist whose shabby world is confined to desk, fridge and bong. The fact is that while he has been busily manufacturing his awe-inspiring mountain of art, he has at the same time, and with no less determination, managed to develop into a swinger of exceptional charm and dignity. And while it is of course foolish to presume too much with regard to any artist's self-revelations, I believe I can allege, among what are surely my rather few legitimate introductory remarks, that here and there among the pages of the present volume the attentive reader will be pleased to find the origins of this swingerhood well and amusingly intimated.

Obviously, *But I Like It* does not concern itself with the unique examinations of history and injustice by which Sacco's place in literature would be eventually cemented. However, it can be anticipated that it ought to assume an important role for future Sacco researchers, for in compiling these lesser-known milestones of his journey alongside the rock quasi-culture it can only help to establish a more complete chronology of his development.

"Portrait of the Young Man as a Young Man" and "Portrait of the Artist as an Aging Lightnin' Hopkins Enthusiast" seem to have suggested themselves as tidy bookends to this enterprise.

The former is an over-the-top satire from which Sacco has deliberately deleted any but the bluntest of observations. His brutal sub-

culture caricature identifies the newly-emerged cliché inventively enough and his rendering of the attire is precise. There's little sense of the inside joke here, however: it's not the hipsters but rather the uninformed mass of weekly newspaper readers that he's taking by the hand through the reprehensible shorts-over-longjohns fad. In this way he targets not only the ostensible subject of his mockery — the slovenly grunge-rock clone — but the fact of a degraded and unsophisticated medium in general. The reader is allowed such assumptions, but the words that begin and end this strip,

> *Ten years have passed and it's time to take stock*

and

> *The years are slipping by*[1]

argue that Sacco intends to impress us with a more universal truth. It's a sentiment to which he frequently returns in the strips assembled here, even those that represent what obviously must be regarded as among the least serious of his works.

The "Lightnin' Hopkins" comic opens ten years later, and depicts Sacco's skepticism of his own by now confident and well-honed public image. As before, and with the rest of this book, the topic is music, though if there is an object of satire it is by now apparently Sacco's own equivocal will to self-assurance. While this strip uses a conceit Hollywood has made familiar — seeing the hero's idol manifested as an advice-giving apparition — in comic form it seems novel, especially as it's explained by Sacco's having found in the blues something more than just a fan's obsession. To him, the blues is a form of music that, unlike the puerile rock'n'roll, can stand up to adult scrutiny and mirror adult themes. For Sacco, the vitality of blues is timeless and of Biblical gravity. I infer from various statements he's made (in private conversation) that this relentless music actually enhances his own cartooning stamina.

This ironic portrayal of the sophisticated, well-dressed television interviewee serves as an unironic answer to questions posed in much of Sacco's work from the rock years. Throughout *But I Like It* we see his frequent use of the twin themes of success and jealousy, played for classic underdog laughs: the underground cartoonist bemoaning the cheap glory garnered by the underground rock musician. Railing bitterly about others' undeserved and pointless acclaim was both funny enough, and felt truly enough, for Sacco to return to it again and again.

The second strip prefacing this volume, "Rockin' Rose City," for example, finds Sacco stepping into the pages of his hometown weekly to portray the local alternative-rock absurdity as a direct affront to his own sensitivity and hard work. Of interest is that here we find Sacco in 1994, perhaps only close enough to success to feel the likelihood of it slipping from his grasp, leaving him nothing but his talent and years of unrewarded struggle, yet still he anticipates

> *swallowing his bitterness and pressing on.*[2]

In fact, a mere year or so later he will announce to a few of his friends his intention to quit comics and become a math teacher, as in terms of both dignity and nutrition the pressure of poverty has become nearly too much.

The Miracle Workers' 'Live at the Forum' gatefold cover. They came, they saw, they overdubbed.

Some years earlier, as he begins to develop his rock-cartoonist sideline, the pressure is evidently easier to bear, as for the young the stakes are always lower. Or at least less clearly laid out. "In the Company of Long Hair" (comprising the second issue of Sacco's solo magazine *Yahoo*, and reunited here with its prelude story) demonstrates his facility with sharp comedic journalism, in this case applied to a little-known mid-'80s retro-rock milieu.

His participatory narrative of a tour through Europe takes place in an un-globalized era where alternative-rock hasn't yet superseded the Cold War as the primary engine of geopolitics. The situation bestows upon him limitless opportunities to mock the band-members' preposterous reality deficit, some of which are taken along the way, but the climactic freakout scene disregards the meritless entertainers as Sacco's frustrated desire for some swinging depravity of his own pushes them literally off the margins of the page. Together with the ensuing flashback to an episode in West Berlin, this outrageous sequence is a masterpiece of graphic control in which Sacco's layout expertly propels the reader through a whirling, surreal hysteria of tequila-spun party-chasing.

The tour is the first of Sacco's many significant encounters with rock culture and its endless provision of tedium, and that the novelty hasn't worn off is apparent. The story is made up almost entirely of uninvented details and moments, elements Sacco finds of interest as he records what is to him a not yet familiar reality. Long drives, sadistic border police, nightclub squalor, lazy musical pretension — he'd get fed up with the rock scene's latent self-importance soon enough, but the tone in this strip is often one of fondness, of a satirist agreeably beguiled by his subject.

Notable as well is the fact that "In the Company of Long Hair" finds Sacco dealing with a rock aesthetic that he can still relate to his own tastes in music, which at the time run very much in favor of classic psychedelia.

Eventually, Sacco would take on the role of obsessed fan to write about the Rolling Stones; an equally profound bemusement would, by the end of the decade, lead to his documenting another tour, this time with the Fat Possum artists. Like the *Yahoo* strip, such stories will demonstrate a genial engagement with the subject at hand. In the years 1990-1993, however, income from his comics, including the magazine version of *Palestine*, is modest, and to make ends meet he begins to produce numerous gag strips, mostly sold to European music periodicals.

The genial touch, and indeed the documentary impulse, is largely absent from these grunge-era satires. Here Sacco is at his best either when, as in too few instances, he uses himself as a character, or when fairly ignoring music altogether. We now see that the more creatively-rendered strips of this period tend to be those to which the rock-music theme is least relevant. It seems likely that during this period (when his facility with more serious, full-length work has begun to be explored) Sacco's interest in rock'n'roll as subject matter has already begun to wane. In most of these strips he apparently regards it as undeserving of observant commentary. Here, the tendency is to place contemporary rock characters and situations subordinate to the absurd, monumentally-

Tour poster. When in doubt, draw things smashing things.

Drawing on the jacket of a test pressing of the Miracle Workers' "Live at the Forum."

scaled gags of his own feverish imagination.

In any event, this is the early '90s, and though he may wish otherwise, Sacco can hardly maintain complete immunity to the current of belief that has by this time come to govern all youth and art subcultures. Somewhere around the turn of the decade tremendous advances are made in the science of market exploitation; the result is that a sort of mandate springs into being, insisting that nothing — neither history, nor politics, nor '60s psychedelia — can matter more than the making of alternative lemons into lucrative mainstream lemonade. Cultural power is now wielded by an increasingly pitiless, not to mention loud, regime. Of course, Sacco's interest in anything resembling alternative rock culture has begun and ended rather a long time before. By roughly 1993 his proximity to the alternative music business has forced him to witness too much unpleasantness, and he evidently reaches the conclusion that rock has become insufficiently suited to his more recent developments with regard to larger themes of adulthood and uncertainty.

Presently, even as he has found rock culture conclusively lacking in material for his humor, discourse, and revelation, Sacco finds himself obliged to draw inspiration from his own ongoing personal obsession with the Rolling Stones. Occasioned by the Stones' album releases and tours of the mid- and late-'90s, the series "The Stones and I" and "Suffering for the Stones" are each a brilliant, preposterous amalgam of elegy, ode and satire. As we've seen, Sacco only rather cursorily ever employs anything resembling an inside joke in his grunge-themed work, which generally incorporates few arcane details. In the Stones material, by contrast, obscure references and unusual lyric quotes make clear by their abundance that he relishes this scholarship, and indeed is thoroughly delighted by his own idolatry for the band.

At the beginning of the Stones cycle, Sacco positions himself for eventual transformation. In the first two strips, the desperate rock-scene present, in which he's made himself a laughingstock, forces him to admit that he's as yet utterly unable to age with dignity. This, as well as his distant, Beatle-adoring past, seems to have given way to an emotional void from which total devotion to the Stones is somehow the only way out. He proclaims, standing at a gravestone reading "Hope,"

> *To embrace the Stones is to acknowledge something else is all but played out and dead in myself.*

Then, strapped into the car on the way to the concert he continues,

> *On the other hand, maybe it's only rock'n'roll.*[3]

By the last of the Stones comics he and his fellow believers have come closer to achieving the sort of adult dignity Sacco notices so infrequently among his peers. Or at least, they seem to have gone slightly upscale, as under their scrutiny the behemoth band's outlandish longevity somehow both affirms and assuages the dreadful inevitability of middle age.

Of course, the Stones, and their many cover-versions of blues originals, are what leads Sacco to what by the late '90s he finds he's spent no inconsiderable effort in achieving, that is, a full-blown, record-amassing blues fandom. If

Sacco's personal Stonesmania can be characterized as an eleventh-hour attempt to stave off his dotage (and we can say with confidence that it *can*), his obsession with the blues represents something like reconciliation with the certainty of old age. As the century ends, so does Sacco's resistance to the final ingredient of dignity: that youth must not only willingly but in fact eagerly be left behind. And if he finds that the Stones are breathtakingly old, still they're only as old as, perhaps, Mt. Rushmore. The blues, he's certain, are old as the tombs of the Egyptian kings.

Thus, amid frequent pursuit of ever-more obscure blues artists, and funded by the commercial success which in this period begins to gain traction, Sacco weds his avocation and profession to spectacular effect in "The Rude Blues." Readers familiar with his more serious work will notice the similarly precise illustration style (though, atypically, enhanced with earthy color) as well as that of Sacco's respectful text, in which T-Model Ford and the other members of the Fat Possum roster do most of the talking. More direct remarks by Sacco on his personal relationship to the blues genre are found in the Lightnin' Hopkins strip that follows.

The inclusion in this volume of "The Rude Blues" serves well enough as an example of where traditional lines, distinguishing Sacco's serious works from what might be called (to use a term of Graham Greene's coinage) his "entertainments," can be seen to blur. Sacco has come to be admired for having elevated serious comics with his carefully drawn and written reportage, and for having given his medium a previously unsought historical weight. Nonetheless his modern reader would do well to observe that such distinctions — between the foreign-correspondent and the gag-writer, between serious and silly — will in the case of this particular artist encourage an incomplete critical understanding.

Directing himself toward documentary truth, of course, has frequently motivated Sacco to include himself in that truth, but to a degree that varies according to the needs of the story. We can observe that the tentacles of autobiography reach thinnest into the more serious of his journalism comics, and wrap themselves thicker around the minor, and in some cases, the more frivolous works. And so it is often in these, as we see in *But I Like It*, that the chronology taking him from long-haired diffidence to eventual well-groomed mastery is the more explicitly found, for it is here that his impulse toward self-revelation is most liberated. The rock comics provide this in useful outline. Early on, an alternative-rock hegemony on the horizon, he's counting his pennies to be a paying customer of rock'n'roll's adolescent sideshow. Later, still penniless, he's worked his way up to guest-list semi-insider. By decade's end he's buying dinners for impoverished record labels (and, one is fairly sure, selecting decent wines). His professionalism fully ripened, his life and artistry are now of equal and incontrovertible vigor.

Until such time as a satisfactory Sacco biography appears, it is his readers' obligation to find the artist revealed only from what is implicit in the published works. Fortunately, by close examination of what he's seen fit to produce in the way of secondary projects such as those collected here, we are allowed yet greater access to his complex motives, beliefs and tastes, and we provide ourselves with yet brighter illumination of his astonishing, manifold accomplishments.

ENDNOTES:

1. But I Like It, p. vi
2. p. viii
3. p. 109

Clockwise from top-left: Gerry Mohr, Matt Rogers, Robert Butler, and Gene Trautmann.

SHAME AND LOATHING

INTRODUCTION BY JOE SACCO

FROM MY VANTAGE POINT, perched on the very middle rung of middle age, a little gassy and liable to nod off after dinner but backed by full liquor and medicine cabinets and festooned with the laurels of my innumerable successes, I look back with neither tear nor sigh, in fact only because dollars have swapped hands, at the creature I was as a youth: long-haired, disrespectful, self-righteously if not purposefully impoverished, and half-crazed about rock and roll. Oh yes, back then Jim Morrison's every inane utterance mattered very much to me; I could quote his grunts and belches. And I could tell you who played bongos on the third cut of the second side of Led Zeppelin's first record — and why it mattered. You know how boys are: almost willing to lay down their lives over such tidbits, the morons. Well, I was no different.

Eventually, as documented in the following pages, I ran off as a roadie with a neo-psychedelic punk band and eked out a living as a rock artist in Berlin. What was I thinking? I suppose I wanted to be some sort of rock star in my own right, and since I didn't know how to thrash at a guitar, I simply attached myself to the scene in the only way I knew how — by drawing. Oh, I had some laughs in those days, I got my kicks, but I slept on too many floors and couches, and I stayed up too late too often listening to too many drunk or stoned musicians confide that they, too, were geniuses.

Two or three years later I was finished with the whole music business, because that's what it was — a business, populated with bullshit artists, hangers-on, wide-eyed idiots, some genuinely talented people, and, forever circling and watching, the sharks. Unfortunately, this is my story as much as it is theirs.

Joe Sacco
2006

A desperate plea for work while I scanned the streets of Berlin for cigarette butts.

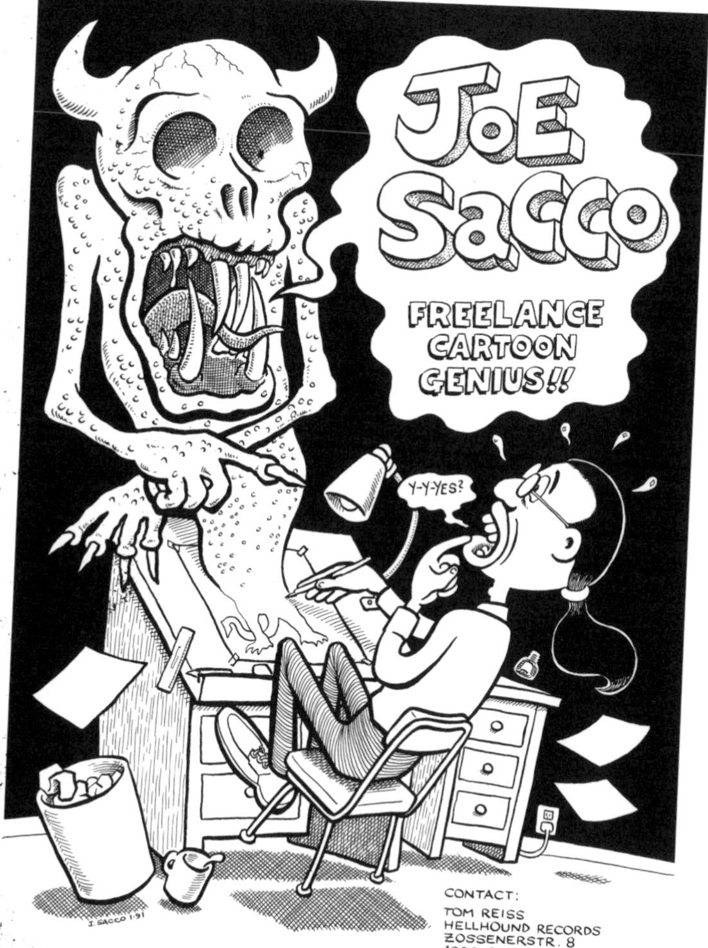

A SIDE: ROAD TRIP

BACK IN 1988, I called my old high school and college chum, Gerry Mohr, who, incidentally, has written the intro to this volume, to ask if I could accompany his band — the Miracle Workers — on its forthcoming European tour. I told him I wanted to document the trip in comics form. Sure, he said, if I sold T-shirts along the way. I didn't think to ask to be compensated; I didn't realize that T-shirt salesman was normally a well-paid position. I thought he was doing me an enormous favor, that bastard.

Anyway, "In The Company Of Long Hair" details the six-week jaunt, the closest I came to the depravity associated with no-holds-barred rock and roll. Those of you who have been following my work for years — hello? HELLO?? — will recall that the story originally appeared in *Yahoo*, my ill-fated and soon-forgotten comics series. Later, "Long Hair" was collected in *Notes From A Defeatist*, a disastrous effort to anthologize my early, funny material and sell it to the intellectuals and revolutionaries who'd bought *Palestine*.

Since no one bought *Yahoo* or *Notes From A Defeatist*, we — that is, my publisher Kim Thompson and I — figured it was safe to repackage "Long Hair" again. Of course, we do so knowing that the few of you who have already seen this story will moan and groan. But to induce you to part with your money anyway, we've added some stuff that turns the "Long Hair" section into a story cycle of sorts. Or that's what the cue cards I'm reading tell me.

"The Search For Credibility" was drawn after "Long Hair," but it takes place in Los Angeles a day or two prior to the European tour. This piece appeared in a Berlin magazine special about music. I wrote it in English, it was translated into German (which I don't read), and that German was eventually translated into French (for a slimmer edition of this book called *Le Rock Et Moi*). Since my English-language notes have long since vanished, I've had to work with translations from the French (via the German) to reconstruct the story back into English. So if the story ends up reading like Esperanto, you'll know why.

Also included are a few pages from my sketchbooks from the tour. I very purposefully left my camera behind to hone my drawing skills, and, as you can see, I spent just as much time jotting down what the band members were saying as I did sketching them. (Let's face it, I've always been a journalist at heart.) Anyway, I am not one of those cartoonists whose every doodle is worthy of publication, and these represent the best pages from the sketch pads. None of these pages has seen print before.

The two pages titled "The Top" were an abortive effort to do a running weekly comic detailing Gerry's move back to Portland, Oregon, some years after the Miracle Workers imploded and he was trying to break his junk addiction. I meant to color them. I only got two of these done, and they've never appeared anywhere before, either.

THE SEARCH FOR
CREDIBILITY
(A ROCK 'N' ROLL STORY OUT OF HOLLYWOOD)
JOE SACCO ©1991
IN TWO DAYS GERRY'S BAND FLIES TO EUROPE.
EEEK! YOU'RE SUPPOSED TO BE A ROCK STAR?! YOU'VE GOT THE SEX APPEAL OF MOTHER TERESA!
THE OUTFIT IS EVERYTHING. LET'S CHECK OUT THE THRIFT SHOPS ON MELROSE BOULEVARD.
IT'S A QUESTION OF CREDIBILITY. GERRY CAN'T HOPE TO TURN ON HIS FANS WITHOUT THE RIGHT LOOK.
PRECISELY. HE NEEDS TO PROJECT EXACTLY WHAT THEY'RE EXPECTING FROM A GARAGE ROCKER.
Girls! Girls! Girls! AND LIQUOR
BEER!
Max's House of Food
J. SACCO 5-91

1.

NOT TIGHT ENOUGH, GERRY. IT WON'T DO.
I'D LIKE TO BUY BOTH PAIRS OF PANTS, BUT THEN I WON'T HAVE A DIME LEFT FOR A SHIRT AND BOOTS.
GERRY!
I THOUGHT YOU WERE ON TOUR IN EUROPE.
IN TWO DAYS.
A EUROPEAN TOUR! HOW COOL!
AHHH... YOU STILL WORKING HERE?
NOTICE HOW SHE TRIES TO ESTABLISH HER FAMIL-IARITY WITH GERRY.
SHE BELIEVES HER CREDIBILITY IN THE HOLLYWOOD SCENE WILL BE ENHANCED BY A PUBLIC DISPLAY OF PHYSICAL INTIMACY WITH A LOCAL ROCK FIGURE.
DID YOU WANT TO BUY THOSE PANTS?
J. SACCO '91
2.

HEY! I GOT TWO PAIRS OF PANTS FOR 20 BUCKS!
SURPRISED? SHE'D HAVE SOLD THEM TO YOU FOR TEN, JUST SO SHE COULD SAY YOU WERE HER CUSTOMER.
A GOOD POINT. SCENESTERS BUILD THEIR CREDIBILITY BASED ON THE CREDIBILITY OF THE PEOPLE THEY CLAIM TO KNOW.
Beverly Hills
i missed the Bus.
WE'RE IN AGREEMENT. IT'S IMPORTANT THAT GERRY REMAIN FAMOUS SO THAT WE, HIS FRIENDS, CAN SHARE IN THAT FAME.
EXACTLY. THAT'S OF THE UTMOST IMPORTANCE. NOT THAT I'M SLEEPING WITH HIM BECAUSE OF HIS CELEBRITY. I LOVE HIM, OF COURSE.
OF COURSE.
GERRY!
HI! YOU STILL WORKING HERE?
"NO FEET, NO SERVICE"
SALE
Doc Ma
WOW! YOUR T-SHIRT IS BRILLIANT! WHERE DID YOU FIND THAT T-SHIRT?
WHAT DO YOU THINK?
BY KISSING GERRY'S ASS, SHE HOPES TO ELICIT A POSITIVE RESPONSE ON HIS PART, AND PARLAY THAT INTO AN INCREASE IN HER OWN CREDIBILITY.
IT'S ENDLESS!
GOD! THEY SUIT YOU PERFECTLY!
J. SACCO 5·91
3.

HEY! SHE BROUGHT THE PRICE DOWN TO $50!
THERE MIGHT BE SOMETHING TO YOUR THEORY ABOUT CREDIBILITY.
SHE PRACTI-CALLY BEGGED ME TO BUY THEM!
SHIT! I CAN BARELY WALK!
THE ONLY THING THAT MATTERS IS YOUR IMAGE. AND THOSE ARE ROCK STAR SHOES, THAT'S A FACT.
I'VE GOT TO GET THESE BOOTS OFF!
YOU'VE GOT TO BE KIDDING! I'M NOT GOING TO BE SEEN WITH YOU WITHOUT YOUR BOOTS THIS FAR UP MELROSE!
GERRY, YOU WON'T JUST BE GAMBLING WITH YOUR CRED-IBILITY. THERE'S OURS AS WELL!
HONK!
GERRY!
NEED A RIDE?
4.
J. SACCO 5-91

I'M ON MY WAY TO PICK UP SOME COKE FOR MY BOSS. I KNOW A GUY WHO'S GOT GOOD, CLEAN STUFF. HE NEVER PASSES OFF OLD SHIT ON ME.
NOTE HOW SHE ADVERTISES HER EASE WITH THE DRUG SCENE.
SHE'S CONCLUDED THAT FLITTING ON THE PERIPHERY OF SEEDINESS ENHANCES HER CREDIBILITY.
WHAT'S NEW?
OH, WELL, LAST NIGHT SOMEONE BROKE INTO MY CAR AND STOLE MY GREEN JACKET.
YOU SHOULD BE DELIGHTED. YOU CAN HARDLY SAY YOU LIVE IN THIS TOWN IF YOUR CAR HASN'T BEEN BROKEN INTO.
THINK OF THE CREDIBILITY FACTOR.
I HADN'T THOUGHT OF THAT.
CALL ME, GERRY!
SURE!
WE ALL KNOW THAT HE'S NOT GOING TO CALL HER, BUT NOW SHE CAN TELL EVERYONE THAT HE PROMISED TO.
J. SACCO 5.91
5.

THIS WOULDN'T BE BAD IN PINK.
GERRY!
REMEMBER ME? I PLAY WITH THE SONS OF SHAPIRO.
THE SONS OF WHA--?
WE OPENED FOR YOU AT THE ANTI-CLUB THE OTHER DAY.
GERRY DOESN'T REMEMBER. THIS GUY IS SUFFERING A SEVERE BLOW TO HIS CREDIBILITY.
YES, BUT PERHAPS THERE ARE PEOPLE WHO DON'T PAY ATTENTION TO THE NOTION.
WOW! CHECK IT OUT! WE'VE GOT THE SAME T-SHIRT! AWESOME!
THE SAME T-SHIRT AS THAT GUY! CHRIST! I CAN'T BELIEVE IT! THIS THROWS GERRY'S CREDIBILITY INTO THE BASEMENT!
AND OURS WITH IT!
6.
J. SACCO 5·91

WE PLACED ALL OUR HOPE FOR CRED-IBILITY IN SOMEONE ELSE, AND SUDDENLY, POOF, IT'S GONE!
I'M GOING HOME TO COLLAPSE IN A COMA.
HEY! WHAT'S UP WITH YOU TWO?
I'M SURE WE DIDN'T BUY OUR T-SHIRTS AT THE SAME PLACE!
HEY!
WAIT FOR ME!
AAAUUUGHHH!
J. SACCO 5.91

7.

Yahoo #2 cover.

This is GERRY...
GERRY hates THE BEATLES,
KNOWS ME TOO WELL...
OKAY, I SAY, I WON'T HUM ANY, SING ANY...
IS THAT IT? THAT THE ONLY PROBLEM?
NO... MIGHT NOT BE ROOM IN THE VAN.
THAT'S A GIGGLE...
ALREADY GIVEN NOTICE ON JOB AND APARTMENT...
ALREADY OVER THE ATLANTIC...
FREE BEER! Y'HEAR THAT, HUTCH? FREE FUCKIN' BEER!
HERE, OL' BOY, HAVE YOURTHELF AN ENGLITH BREAKFATHT...
COME AMSTERDAM, MATT'S SHNOCKERED... HIS SENSE OF DISGUISE GONE BALLS UP...
TIE BACK THE HAIR!
THEY WON'T HASSLE YOU IF YOU TIE BACK THE HAIR...
MINUTES LATER, PASSPORT CONTROL'S MARCHING HIM OFF... NO RETURN TICKET, JUST $31 IN HIS POCKET...
DAYS PASS, MATT STILL PLAYS IT FOR LAUGHS...
TOLD 'EM I'M INNA BAND...
SHOWED 'EM MY CARD...
THAT FUCKER THROWS IT BACK IN MY FACE.
TOLD 'EM I'M AN AMERICAN...
AND THEY FUCKIN' SLAM ME IN THE COOLER.
FUCKIN' DUTCH CUNTS!
WE ALL LAUGH HARD, ME THE HARDEST... IT'S MY $1550 THAT BAILS MATT OUT... NOT THAT I EVER HOLD IT OVER ANYONE'S HEAD... HUH, BOYS?
BOYS?
I GOTTA RIGHT
J. SACCO 12-88

The SWEET, ISN'T THAT A HOT NAME? The SWEET, IT ROLLS LOVINGLY OFF GERRY'S TONGUE... MUSIC MACHINE, Motörhead, DOESN'T everyone DIG ♫The Ace of ♠♫?... HEY, ARE WE STILL GONNA DO ♫All Sold Out♫?... LAST NIGHT'S GIG WAS EINSTEIN, SAYS MATT ...'I DREAM OF GENIE'... 'HOGAN, THERE ARE REPORTS YOU WERE SEEN IN BERLIN'...
'MEMBER THAT BRADY BUNCH WHERE THEY GO TO HAWAII?
JAN IN A MICRO-BIKINI... IT WAS A TOTAL BONER ...I JACKED OFF FOR WEEKS AFTER THAT EPISODE!
MARSHA WAS A DOG THOUGH.
Y'THINK ALICE AND THE BUTCHER EVER BONED?
First SPASM PASSES... SO, TOO, A VILLAGE, A MOUNTAIN, A HERD OF GOATS...
HUTCH THE SOUND ENGINEER ROLLS A FATTIE
Matt EXAMINES A KALEIDOSCOPIC ROADBONER
SUDDENLY
WHADDOYABLOW?
PUSSY!
WHAT'SUPYERBUTT?
SHIT!
WHADDOYASUCK?
DICK!
THAT'S RIIIGHT!!
Dickhall... RAPID QUESTIONS, SIMULTANEOUS RESPONSES... I'VE SEEN IT LAST TWO HOURS... ANOTHER OF ROBERT'S QUESTIONABLE CONTRIBUTIONS TO THE VAN LEXICON...
DICK!
UH... PUSSY!
SHIT!
EVEN GERRY'S SUCKED IN... GIGGLING, HE CAN'T KEEP UP, NOPE, NOT WITH THE 21 YEAR OLDS... SINKS BACK SUDDENLY REFLECTIVE... THINGS ARE GETTING STINKY...
I THINK WE SHOULD INSIST ON BEING LED BY HAND TO A LAUNDROMAT.
HEY, I GOTTA PEE!
NEXT RESTSTOP, SAYS LURCH, TWENTY KILOMETERS...
J. SACCO 12-88

WHERE ARE WE ANYWAY?
LURCH, YOU GOT THAT MAP OF EUROPE?
HE'S GERMAN, AIN'T HE?
HAHA! GERMANS ALWAYS GOT MAPS OF EUROPE...
EUROPE, THE WAR, WHICH WAR? ROBERT WOULD LIKE A DISCUSSION OF THE LAST ONE... FALL OF FRANCE IN '40... THE KURSK SALIENT... MATT'S ON ABOUT SS ATROCITIES, THE ZODIAC KILLER, CHARLIE MANSON... THIS BESTSELLER ON THE NEWEST SERIEL KILLER SUCKS, WARNS HE...
IT'S TOTALLY BOGUS.
The SWEET SAYS GERRY LOV. ING. LY...
WHAT SONGS D'THEY DO?
LIGHTS
PENCILS
DIPPED IN SHIT, THE STARES ANSWER... BEST STICK TO MY JOB...
COOPERATION IS TOTAL... TOTAL, MAN...
ACTION!!
MATT OPENS GOB FOR THESE SKETCHES OF HIS BROKEN TOOTH...
GENE DROPS LEATHER PANTS FOR THIS QUICKIE OF HIS BUTT PROBLEM...
EVEN THE DISH WHO GETS LAID IN HEIDELBERG KNOWS TO SMILE FOR THE SOFT LEAD PENCIL...
WE DIDN'T BRING A PHOTO-GRAPHER...
...WE BROUGHT A CARTOON-IST.
GENE BUYS ME PENCILS, VOLUNTEERS IDEAS FOR THE COMIC...
LIKE NOT USING A RUBBER...
...AND HAVING YOUR DICK FALL OFF.
HEY, GENE, AIN'T YOU READING 'MODERN DRUMMER' OR SOMETHING ???
J. SACCO 12·88

ONLY ROBERT, THAT PROTO-LOWEST COMMON DENOMINATOR, CUTS A MENTAL FART MY WAY...
YOU AN' YOUR SKETCHBOOK... YOU MUST THINK YOU'RE PRETTY HOT, HUH?
YEAH, I'M HOT, ROBERT, DON'T NEED TO SHAKE ASS ON-STAGE TO KNOW SO, SO FUCK YOU, WE ALL KNOW YOU'RE #4 ON THE GERMAN INDEPENDENTS, HOW ALL THE WAY-COOL HOLLYWOOD SKIRT LINES UP AT THE SCREAM...
WE'VE ALL HEARD THE STORY HOW GERRY MET SLY STONE
AND THE ONLY REASON I'M TRYING MATT'S LEATHER JACKET BACKSTAGE NAPLES IS 'CAUSE HE INSISTS...
YIIIIHAA... WHAT'S HAPPENING AFTER THE SHOW, SWINGER?
HOW MUCH WAS IT?
BUT NOT LISTENING TO THE ANSWER, TOO BUSY ASKING THE QUESTIONS, TOO BUSY GETTING IT DOWN, MAN... I'M ONTO SOMETHING, EVERYONE KNOWS IT...
OF COURSE... THERE'S ONLY SO MUCH MILEAGE YOU CAN GET BEING RESIDENT CARTOONIST...
AND AS MUCH AS THE FELLAHS DIG ME, DIG THE SKETCHES... AS MUCH BAIL MONEY AS I COUGHED UP... (WHICH I NEVER HOLD OVER ANYONE'S HEAD)
...THERE'S NOTHING IN WRITING...
OUCH!
WATCH THE FUCKIN' HAIR.
SORRY.
CAN WE MOVE THE LEG, GENE?
J. SACCO 12-88
I'VE SEEN GOOD BOTTLES OF SCOTCH GET JETTISONE

SO, OKAY, KNOW WHAT I'LL DO, I'LL SELL T-SHIRTS, YEAH, JUST DON'T CALL ME DEADWEIGHT, HELL, I LIKE MEETING PEOPLE...
YOU HAVE FREE T-SHIRT FOR ME?
T-Shirts 20 DM
PROBLEM IS, THIS LOT'S NEVER SEEN ITS SHARE OF THE MARSHALL PLAN...
I'M BULLIED INTO REDUCING PRICES, BLUDGEONED INTO GIVING IT AWAY ...SURRENDER UNCONDITIONAL ...THEY CLEAN ME OUT, BLOW MY NOSE... I BARELY ESCAPE WITH MY FILL-INGS ...
MEANWHILE, ELECTRIC WARRIORS DESCEND FROM BACKSTAGE, TOWELLED OFF, GLOWING TRANSCENDENT...
THE CROWD GASPS... EYES ROLL UP, KNEES WOBBLE, PANTIES MOISTEN ...FATIMA NIGHT AFTER NIGHT.
SO, JOE, HOW'D WE DO?
FUCKIN' HOT, GERRY... YOU OUTDID YOURSELF... YOU OUT-STOOGED IGGY... YOU--
I MEAN, HOW'D WE DO WITH T-SHIRTS?
T-SHIRTS... BAH! T-SHIRTS IS A FRONT!! THEY KNOW WHY I'M HERE, I KNOW WHY I'M HERE, YOU KNOW WHY I'M HERE, LET'S FUCKING GET ON WITH IT...
J. SACCO 12-88

HE CALLED THE DOCTOR
THE VAN'S GONE GOOEY... SQUISHY TISSUES ANKLE DEEP, A TRAIL OF SNOT SINCE GRONINGEN... (AND YOU SHOULD SEE SOME OF HIS PILLOW CASES.)
FUCKIN', THAT IS SICK! YOU ARE THE SICKEST MOTHERFUCKER I KNOW!
SORRY.
CAN'T YOU AT LEAST CLEAR THE VAN?
DORTMUND IN PRACTICALLY CALLING FOR A PRIEST... BY MÜNSTER HE'S FLIRTING WITH RIGOR MORTIS...
MY VOICE IS COMPLETELY GONE.
PROBABLY PERMANENTLY DAMAGED.
THIS TOUR WAS A BIG FUCKING MISTAKE.
WE SHOULD HAVE STAYED IN L.A.
I CAN'T EVEN CONCEIVE OF SINGING IN BERLIN TONIGHT.
SO WHY SING?
BLOND PRETTIES LICK LIPS, HEAD-BANGERS SLAM REGARDLESS...
THEIR GONGS BANGED, THEY'VE ALREADY ARRIVED WHERE THEY'RE GOING. GERRY COULD FART THE NUMBERS FOR ALL THEY CARE...
HELL, MIGHT SAVE HIS PIPES...
COUPLE OF SHOWS CANCELLED ...WE HANG OUT, EATING POMMES FRITES, WASHING HAIR...
HEY! LET'S CHECK OUT THE WALL!
GERRY DON'T BUDGE...
TURNS OUT IT'S JUST AN INFECTION... NASTY ONE, NO DOUBT, BUT NO MATCH FOR KICK-ASS PHARMACEUTICALS...
GERRY BRIGHTENS UP... HE'S READY TO PICK UP WHERE HE LEFT OFF...
JUST BEFORE I FUCKED UP MY THROAT, I STARTED TO GET INTO THIS DRUNK THING.
WE FINISH OUR COFFEE AND PILE BACK INTO THE VAN.
J. SACCO 12·88

Looking at you
SOME-TIMES THEY WAVE YOU THROUGH... USUALLY, THOUGH, THEY DON'T GROOVE ON THE HAIR.
SCHEISSE!
STOP
Weiterfahrt nach Aufforderung
SPANIARDS SNEER, ASK WHAT YOU'RE SMOKING...
ITALIANS MAKE YOU WAIT, CHECKING EVERYONE TWICE EVER SINCE HANNIBAL AND HIS ELEPHANTS SLIPPED THROUGH...
EAST GERMANS GIGGLE AT PASSPORT SMILES: THAT REALLY YOU?
BAVARIANS MAKE HUTCH SHAKE OUT HIS DREADLOCKS...
THEY EMPTY OUT TRASH...
SNIFF
SNIFF
BRING ON THE DOGGIE.
NOW THEY'RE GOING THROUGH HIS CASE... WE'RE HANGING AROUND, WORD IN THE VAN HAS IT LURCH KEEPS NUDIE SHOTS OF HIS GIRL IN THERE...
WHAT A MORON, LURCH IS CARRYING NOSE CANDY PARAPHERNALIA...
THEY TAKE HIM AWAY, GIVE HIM THE RUBBER GLOVE TREATMENT...
SPEX
THE BAVARIANS DON'T FIND THE NUDIE SHOTS.
IF ONLY IT'D BEEN THE SWISS FRONTIER... WHEN IT COMES TO EFFICIENCY, THE SWISS TAKE THE STRUDEL.
J. SACCO 12.88

COME ON. LET'S JUST GET TO THE CLUB. THERE'LL BE FOOD BACK-STAGE.
FUCKIN', THERE WON'T BE CHEESE-BURGERS BACK-STAGE.
LURCH!
STOP THE VAN! SLAM ON THE BRAKES! ARCH ME!!
FIVE MINUTES AGO I WAS A VEGETARIAN... NOW I'M SITTING HERE EATING A MacRIB...
I HATE YOU FOR DOING THIS TO ME.
FUCKIN', I DIDN'T SPEND YOUR 12 MARKS, DID I?
MMMM... PEPSI ME.
YOU CONFUSE BEING BUMMED FOR NOT BEING DRUNK.
AFTER CRUISING THROUGH THE PRADO YOU DON'T BELIEVE IN JESUS?
I BELIEVE IN ADVERTISING.
THERE ARE MORE PAINTINGS OF ELVIS ON VELVET THAN THERE ARE OF JESUS.
I BET THE FUZZTONES NEVER GO TO ART MUSEUMS.
EVERYWHERE I FUCKING GO THE COPS BUM ME OUT...
PRETTY SOON I WON'T BE ABLE TO WALK...
I'VE GOT A FUCKING WARRANT FOR MY ARREST IN L.A.
FAR OUT.
J. SACCO 1.89

OH MY! and BOOHOO
NO DOUBT, THE ANT THING'S GOT POTENTIAL...
COMPLIMENTING A BABE ON HER THORAX-- COME ON, THAT'S DYNAMITE STUFF...
A WONDER MATT'S SHTICK HASN'T GENERATED ANY ABDOMEN...
TONIGHT, THOUGH...
I KNOW THOSE CHICKS WANNA SWING!
THEY'RE HOT!
I'M GONNA BUTTER UP THEIR BUNS AND SLAP 'EM TILL THEY'RE CHERRY RED!
WHAAACK!
TONIGHT STRINGS SNAP LEFT AND RIGHT...
GENE'S GAP-FILLING WITH SWEATED SOLOS, DRUMMING UP A DARK, PRIMAL SWAMP...
TONIGHT...
SHATTERED GLASS CRACKLES UNDER GERRY'S BOOTS...
HE'S MARCHING TAIL, WALTZING SELF-PARODY...
I LOVE THIS GIRL BECAUSE SHE IS A TOTAL FREAK...
WHAT SAY WE GO BACK TO MY HOTEL ROOM, SHOOT DOPE FOR A WEEK?
Rickenbacker
TONIGHT MATT'S ANTENNAE HANG FLOPPY, SIX-THIRTY...
NOT YET THE HOUR OF THE ANT GAMBIT...
THEY SHOWED UP WITH BOYFRIENDS!
WROOONG!
J. SACCO 12-88

AND TONIGHT SOMETHING SOFT AND SWISS IS TURNING MY HEAD...
EYES PARRY, HOLD, DILATE POSSIBILITY...
BEER?
...ZE M.C.5, ZE STOOGES, JA, VERY MUCH ZE STOOGES.
YEAH, THE STOOGES.
WE BOTH KNOW THE LINES TO THIS CONVER-SATION; SCRIPT'S GOOD ANY NIGHT-CLUB BARCELONA TO BERLIN...
JUST WHEN I'M CALLING FOR CURTAIN, ENTER ROBERT, AFTERSHOW CHATTERING...
WHAT'S THIS SCENE?
WHO WROTE HIS LINES?
HE WASN'T AT REHEARSAL...
THEN ANOTHER TWIST...
HER HAND REACHING FOR MY LAP...
SHE LIFTS MY SKETCHBOOK...
MY SKETCHBOOK...
BEYOND ROAD-CREW I AM...
AND NOW SHE WILL KNOW...
SHE WILL KNOW.
A SKETCHBOOK FLIPPING OVER...
A PLASTIC BAG OPEN-NING, A LIGHTER FLASHING...
SHE IS HEATING HASH ON THE BACK COVER...
J. SACCO 12·88

...UGHING SMOKEY RESIN...
I AM RUNNING LIKE EVERYONE ELSE...
PILING INTO A CAR...
KISSING CEILING...
WHERE'S ROBERT AND THE GIRL?..
I AM RUNNING UP STAIRS...
A PARTY GOING ON...
ESCALATING FLIRTATION TO KEEP THIS TRIANGLE ISOSCELES...
BUT ROBERT'S FORMING NEW ANGLES...
CHASING HER AROUND WITH A PLASTIC CRAB...
ROBERT'S ALREADY THERE, SHAKING TO THE MUSIC, NOT A SELF-CONSCIOUS BONE IN HIS ORANGE COUNTY BODY...
HE'S GOT HER SHAKING...
I GRAB HER HAND...
WE ARE RUNNING DOWN STAIRS...
THEIR LONG HAIR DANCING...
WHERE'D SHE GO?
HERS FLOWS LONG, BUT HIS FLOWS FOREVER, SHIMMERING LIKE THE RHINE...
PILING INTO CARS...
RUNNING UP STAIRS...
A PARTY GOING ON...
YOU GOTTA BE MOVED BY HAIR LIKE THAT... AT THE VERY LEAST, YOU GOTTA STAND ASIDE.
J. SACCO 12·88

TONIGHT WE'RE BACK IN THE VAN, HOTEL-BOUND...
THE SPACEY CHICK BLEW GERRY OFF LONG AGO, HE'S SAYING HE DOESN'T CARE...
I DON'T CARE.
GENE CARES, GENE ALWAYS CARES...
ALL I WANT IS A GIRL TO SHNUGGLE WITH.
THE SADDEST MOMENT TONIGHT
TONIGHT, PARTY RESIDUE LINGERS IN A HOTEL ROOM...
CRASHED OUT, STONED, MUTTERING MONOSYLLABLES IN A FOREIGN LANGUAGE...
JA?
JA.
JA?
DOWNSTAIRS, AN ANT KING HAS HUNG UP HIS CROWN...
BOYFRIENDS!
WRONG.
TOMORROW WE'RE BACK IN THE VAN... THE VAN, A TRUTH MACHINE, IN THE MORNING WE GET ALL THE DETAILS...
NOTHING? NOTHING?
ARE YOU KIDDING? WITH HER? A JUNKY?
WHAT A FUCKING STUD.
TODAY'S ANOTHER TOWN...
ANOTHER TOWN, DIFFERENT CHICKS.
J. SACCO 1·89

UNTOLD FABLES...
LET'S GO NOW ON AN EMPTY STOMACH, WHILE WE'RE MEAN.
LET GERRY DO THE TALKING.
F THE VIXENS
WROOONG!
ALL THESE HAVE MEAT IN THEM.
THERE'S SUPPOSED TO BE TWO VEGETARIAN SANDWICHES BACKSTAGE.
WHAT AM I SUPPOSED TO EAT?
WE WANT FOOD WHEN WE GET TO THE CLUB, NOT JUST BEFORE WE GO ON.
TONY, I DO WANT TO ENFORCE THE 48-BEER POLICY...HAVING TO PAY FOR BEER LAST NIGHT WAS TOTALLY BOGUS.
WE BETTER TAKE THOSE SANDWICHES AND STOW 'EM.
HE DOESN'T WANT TO KISS OUR ASS, AND I DON'T LIKE THAT.
PROMISES DON'T BUY ANYONE A HOT MEAL.
BUT I WILL GET THE 3,200 MARKS TO YOU TOMORROW AND THE OTHER HALF WHEN YOU RETURN.
YOU SAID IN HEIDELBERG YOU OWED US 10,000 MARKS. HOW IS 3,200 HALF OF 10,000?
I WILL SHOW YOU THE BOOKS.
BLOW THOSE BOOKS OUT YOUR ASS.
BUT I'VE BEEN WORKING HARD FOR YOU, I'VE BEEN--
SURE. THE FALL TOUR GETS CANCELLED, OUR REPUTATION IN HOLLAND'S DAMAGED, AND MEANWHILE WE'RE STARVING IN LOS ANGELES.
SHE JUST MISSES THE HUGS AND KISSES.
OUT OF SIGHT, OUT OF MIND.
I BET THE FUZZTONES NEVER HAVE TO PUT UP WITH ANY OF THIS SHIT.
FACE IT, WE'VE GOT SOMEONE WHO'S TOTALLY UP TO HER ASS IN PROJECTS.
I THOUGHT SHE WASN'T THOUGH.
BUT--
YOU FUCKED WITH THE WRONG BAND, AND THIS BAND IS FUCKING BACK.
THE TROUBLE WITH HAVING A FRIEND AS MANAGER IS YOU CAN'T SCREAM AT THEM.
AT LEAST IF YOU'RE GOING TO DEAL WITH SOMEONE'S BULLSHIT, IT SHOULD BE INTERESTING BULLSHIT.
J. SACCO 1-89

LURCH, WANT ME TO DRIVE?
IT'S GOT GLARE ON THE PAGE
HOLD THAT UP... THAT'S NASTY!
EYES ON THE ROAD, MATT
WHY ARE WE STOPPING?
SLIDE THE FUCKIN' DOOR.
WHAAACK!
GERRY'S NEW COMFORT CONCEPT IS STRETCHING OUT ON THE FLOOR
WHO HAS TO PISS?
IS THAT HUTCH SAWING LOGS?
I'M STARTING TO BURN OUT ON BURNING OUT.
WHO HAS TO PISS?
SLIDE THE FUCKIN' DOOR.
GERRY'S NEW COMFORT CONCEPT FAILS
WHY ARE WE STOPPING?
SLIDE THE FUCKIN' DOOR.
I FEEL LIKE A MORON.
ARE WE THERE?
J. SACCO 1-89

THE HOTEL HASN'T HEARD ABOUT ANY RESERVATIONS.
WHAT?
WROOONG.
IT'S NOT LIKE WE CAN STOP ANY-WAY... FUCKIN', WE'LL MISS THE SHOW.
WILL SOMEONE ORANGE JUICE ME?
ANOTHER WARM BEER
LET'S BAG VIGO AND GO TO MADRID ...AT LEAST WE'LL BE RESTED FOR MADRID.
YOU'RE NOT GONNA MAKE MONEY CANCELLING SHOWS.
FUCK, WE'VE BEEN ON THE ROAD 24 HOURS... YOU'VE BEEN ASLEEP... GENE AND I'VE BEEN HELPING LURCH DRIVE.
DRIVE 2,000-PLUS KILOMETERS, PLAY A MIDNIGHT SHOW, LOAD UP, AND GO STRAIGHT TO MADRID -- THAT'S FUCKING CRIMINAL.
ALL RIGHT, IT'S YOUR TOUR.
FUCKIN', WE'RE NOT GONNA MAKE THE SHOW BY HANGING OUT WONDERING IF WE CAN MAKE THE SHOW ...GERRY AND MATT DON'T REALLY WANT TO TRY.
Y'SEEN THE MAP? IT'S SECONDARY ROADS FROM HERE ON, DUDE... I GUESS 12, 16 MORE HOURS... I DIDN'T WANNA SAY ANYTHING, BUT...
Y'GET THROUGH?
Y'SPEAK TO ROBERTO?
YEAH. RELAX, BOYS. WE'RE GOING TO MADRID.
RAIN ON THE PLAIN
KILOMETERS CLICK BY
WHY ARE WE STOPPING?
WHO HAS TO PISS?
SLIDE THE FUCKIN' DOOR.
J. SACCO 1-89

you've got your head on BACKWARDS

MATT'S BEAMING LIKE A BASTARD...

KING OF ALL ANTS THINKS HE'S DONE ME A FAVOR...

SET ME UP WITH MS. ITALIAN NOSE 1988...

WE'RE CHEWING THE USUAL PSYCH-EDELIC CUD...

THIRTEENTH FLOOR ELEVATORS, SI?... CHOCOLATE WATCH BAND?...DO YOU KNOW THE WORDS TO 'MIRACLE WORKER'?

I AIN'T NO MIRACLE WORKER... I'M JUS' AN ORDINARY GUY...

YOU KNOW THE WORDS TO 'I'M NOT LIKE EVERY-BODY ELSE'?

NO, DON'T KNOW THE WORDS...

PLEASE, SHUT THE FUCK UP...

CHRIST, CAN'T GO THROUGH WITH THIS...

I'VE BLOWN IT...

AND NOW THE BLONDE'S MAKING ODD, COOING SOUNDS...

ROBERT READS THE SITUATION LIKE THE WORDS ARE PAINTED RED, TEN FEET HIGH...

JOE, YOU COMIN'?... LET'S GO... COME ON!

I HESITATE, MAYBE I CAN GO THROUGH WITH IT, SHE'S GOT GOOD LEGS...

A TELEPATHIC 'FUCK YOU, THEN,' AND ROBERT'S GONE...

MATT COOKS MY GOOSE...

WHY DON'T YOU TWO RUN ALONG TO THE PANTHEON?

J. SACCO 1-8

I TAKE INVENTORY QUICKLY... THE WHOLE LOT OF THEM SEPARATE ME FROM THE DOOR... SO, IT'S THE BALCONY... FROM THIS HEIGHT, I MIGHT LUCK OUT WITH A SHATTERED ANKLE...
DOOR
ITALIAN GIRL #2
ITALIAN GIRL #1
MATT
ME
BALCONY
THE DOOR OPENS... HUTCH, GENE, LURCH...
WE'RE GOING SOMEWHERE TO EAT... ANYONE COMING?
GENE, M'MAN, HOW'S ABOUT CHECKIN' OUT THE PANTHEON?
NOW? I'M HUNGRY. I HAVEN'T EATEN.
!
HELL, COME ON!
IT'S ROMA, DUDE!
EAT LATER!
I'LL BUY!
LET'S JUS' TAKE A LITTLE OL' STROLL TO THE PANTHEON.
GENE'S A DARLING... GENE, WHO BOUGHT ME SOFT-LEAD PENCILS, ASSENTS...
NOT-QUITE-SOPHIA-LOREN BRIGHTENS UP... I'M ROAD CREW, BUT GENE'S THE DRUMMER, THE REAL THING...
ROMA IS SO NOISY, SO BORING...
I WISH TO GO TO THE STATES...
I LOVE TO MEET THE BANDS ... THE FUZZ-TONES, THE CHESTERFIELD KINGS...
WHEN WE GET TO THE PANTHEON, YOU MEET MY FRIENDS.
BOY OH BOY, WE CAN HARDLY WAIT...
J. SACCO 1·89

IT'S A HALF HOUR WALK...
HER FRIENDS ARE WELL PISSED...
THE PANTHEON IS WELL PISSED ON...
SPEAKING OF, OUR FEMALE COMPANION HAS TO TAKE A WHIZ.
WATCHING HER LEGS WALK OFF...
FUCK, MAYBE I COULD'VE--
I KNEW IT WOULD BE LIKE THIS.
HUH?
I HATE THIS OBLIG-ATION TO ENTERTAIN PEOPLE LIKE HER.
COMES WITH THE TERRITORY, DUDE.
PRICE OF ROCK STARDOM.
YOU GOTTA LET HER DOWN GENTLY.
A FAN WANTS TO MEET THE BAND AND TALK TO THEM.
A GROUPIE WANTS TO HAVE SEX WITH THE BAND...
NOT JUST FUCK ONE GUY FROM ONE BAND, BUT FUCK ALL GUYS FROM ALL BANDS.
Y'SEE THE DIFFERENCE?
YOU'RE A FAN!
ON OUR WAY BACK, HE TRIES...
KNOW WHAT I LIKE ABOUT YOU?
SI? SI?
YOU'RE A FAN, NOT A GROUPIE...
THERE'S A DIFFERENCE.
SHE AIN'T CONVINCED...
I MEAN, THAT'S A GOOD THING!
J. SACCO 1-89

ROBERT. YOUR BASS PLAYING WAS EINSTEIN...
ALL I KNOW IS, I'M STANDING THERE IN FRONT OF PEOPLE AND MY SCENE'S GETTING BLOWN.
I DIDN'T KNOW WHAT YOU WANTED. POINTING TO YOUR EAR AND FLAILING YOUR ARMS DOESN'T MEAN ANYTHING TO ME.
IF WE GET A TALK-BACK MIKE WE GOTTA USE IT.
AS SOON AS YOU TELL ME THERE'S A PROBLEM, I'M ON IT... I JUST CAN'T HANDLE BEING SCREAMED AT.
I'M SORRY I WAS SCREAMING AT YOU... I WAS JUST...
...SCREAMING.
I DIDN'T THINK GERRY WOULD GET THROUGH HIS SUBURBAN CRISIS, BUT TONIGHT HE WAS A STAR...
'CAUSE... IT'S, FUCKIN' ...WHEN I HEAR THAT SONG ...FUCKIN'... I'D LIKE TO KNOW WHAT THAT SONG MEANS.
HOW WILL YOU KNOW TILL YOU PLAY IT? WE'D DO IT RIGHT.
I'M NOT PLAYING IT... IT'S TOO SPECIAL... FUCKIN', IT'S ALREADY PERFECT.
YOU FAG.
FUCK YOU, GERRY!
!
GENE, I FELT PROUD TO STAND IN THE LIGHT OF YOUR METAPHYSICAL DRUMMING...
I SPORTED AN IMMEDIATE ERECTION, WHICH I PROUDLY DISPLAYED TO THE GIRLS.
THIS IS WHERE THEY REALLY MAKE US FEEL IMPORTANT, HUH, GENE?
WE'LL SPLIT IT... YOU JUST HAVE TO KISS OUR ASSES.
WE'LL SPLIT IT.
FUCK YOU.
WE WRITE THE NEXT E.P.
UNTOLD TALES
J. SACCO 1·89

NO FUN TO HANG AROUND

I DIDN'T COME 10,000 MILES TO BE LEFT IN A HOTEL ROOM WHEN THERE'S FUN T'BE HAD.
WRONG WRONG WRONG WRONG
Y'THINK THEY TOOK THE VAN TO FRANKFURT?
NO DOUBT. WHERE THERE'S A U.S. AIR FORCE BASE, THERE'S PUSSY.
OH, YOU SPELL THAT OUT FOR THEM?

I BLAME LURCH FOR THIS. HE KNOWS WE'RE LEAVING AT MIDNIGHT.
THE VAN'S HIS RESPONSIBILITY.
WHAT'S THE STORY ABOUT LEAVING AT MIDNIGHT?
WE SKIPPING OUT ON THE HOTEL BILL?
IT'S MATT'S FAULT. HE CONTROLS LURCH.

I'M HORNY.
I'M BORED.
YOU'RE BORED??! I'M DRINKING WINE!!!
I KNOW OF ZIS BAR VE CAN VALK TO.

GROOVY.
WALL-TO-WALL STONE-WASH.
PRETTY SOON WE'RE GONNA GET INTO A CONVERSATION ABOUT GARFIELD.

THIS IS SORT OF AN INTERESTING LITTLE TOWN, GERRY...
YOU KNOW THAT GUY WHO WROTE THAT BOOK ABOUT THE THIRTY YEARS WAR? 'THE ADVENTURES OF SOMEONEOROTHER'?
NO.
WELL, HE WAS BORN HERE.
J. SACCO 1-89

DON'T GET ME WRONG... I MEAN, FUCKIN', I *LIKE* WALKING AROUND GERMANY WITH YOU GUYS...
BUT I'M HORNY...
JESUS, ALL THAT TAIL THAT'S THROWN ITSELF YOUR WAY, AND YOU DIDN'T DO NOTHIN'... NOT THAT I SHOULD TALK... I HAVEN'T EXACTLY BEEN A SWING MACHINE...
I KNOW. YOU SUCK.

HEY, LOOK... THE VAN... THEY'RE BACK.
OKAY, EVERYONE, LET'S GIVE 'EM THE SILENT TREATMENT.

WHERE THE FUCK WERE YOU?!
DIDN'T YOU FUCKIN' KNOW WE HAD TO LEAVE BY MIDNIGHT?!
FUCK YOU.

REMEMBER...
THE SILENT TREATMENT.
I ♡ ASPRIN
HEY, GERRY? GERRY?
GENE? IS GENE THERE?

I JUST WANNA TELL YOU SOMETHING, THAT'S ALL.

J SACCO '89

COME ON!
COOL OUT!
COOL OUT!

WHERE'D YOU GO? TELL US. TELL US.
WE JUST GOT SOMETHING TO EAT AND THEN TOOK A SIGNED RECORD TO A CLUB IN FRANKFURT, HAD A BEER, AND CAME BACK...
WHAT'S THE FUCKING BIG DEAL?

WHY DIDN'T YOU TELL ANYONE?
I DIDN'T KNOW YOUR FUCKING ROOM NUMBERS...
NO ONE FUCKING TOLD ME ANYTHING WHEN YOU ALL SPLIT THIS MORNING...

WELL, I JUST DON'T LIKE BEING STRANDED IN AN ISOLATED GERMAN VILLAGE ON A NIGHT OFF.
PIKE SAID HE COULD'VE GOT US INTO THE WAS NOT WAS CONCERT IN FRANKFURT.
GERRY DIDN'T HAVE TO FUCKING YELL AND SLAM THE DOOR.

WELL, THE YELLING AND SLAMMING WENT BEYOND WHAT WE'D DISCUSSED.
WE WERE ALL SORT OF PISSED OFF, BUT WE WANTED TO FUCK WITH YOUR MIND A LITTLE TO MAKE IT LOOK LIKE WE WERE REALLY PISSED OFF.
FUCKIN', CAN WE JUST FUCKIN' FORGET IT??!

HEY, MATT?
WHAT?
WHADDOYAGOT?
PUSSY.
THAAAT'S RIIIGHT!!
J. SACCO 1-89

NOTHING MORE TO SAY
I'M SO SICK OF THAT...
I'M SO SICK OF WORKING FOR FREE...
I CAN'T IMAGINE WHAT IT MUST BE LIKE FOR YOU...
YOU'VE BEEN DOING IT FOR YEARS.
Y'GET USED TO IT.
THEY TOLD US WE'D BE STOKED IF WE BROKE EVEN.
I SHOULD'VE KNOWN THINGS WERE BAD WHEN I GOT BUSTED IN HOLLAND AND MY TOOTH BROKE... IT WAS ALL DOWNHILL FROM THERE.
HOW IS YOUR TOOTH?
THE PACKINGTH COMING OUTTH.
EVERYTHING WILL BE ALL RIGHT.
'EVERYTHING WILL BE ALL RIGHT'...
THANKS, MOM.
WE MADE A RECORD DEAL...
PROMOTED THE ALBUM...
CLEANED UP SOME BUSINESS.
MADE SOME NEW FRIENDS...
LEARNED A FEW GERMAN PHRASES...
GOT OUT OF L.A. FOR A GOOD, LONG TIME.
SAW SPAIN.

J. SACCO 1-89

SLOW DEATH
I SAID, 'I'M GONNA USE A RUBBER,' AND SHE SAID, 'WHAT'S THE PROBLEM, DO YOU HAVE AIDS?' AND I SAID, 'NO, IT'S JUST SOMETHING YOU DO, LIKE WEARING A SEATBELT'... SO, ANYWAY, SHE CLIMBS ON TOP, AND AFTER I CAME SHE KEPT RIGHT ON BUCKING...
I HATE IT WHEN GIRLS DO THAT...
JUST WHEN YOU'RE GOING LIMP AND SENS-ITIVE, AND YOU WANT TO EAT A SANDWICH...
YEECH.
FACE IT, LADS, THESE ROCK 'N' ROLL FUCKEROOS HAVE ALL THE WARMTH OF THE LAST ICE AGE.
YOU OUGHTA KNOW, HUH?
THOSE CHICKS ARE SCENE JUNKIES, AND YOU'RE JUST THE LATEST LOT OF LONG-HAIRED NEANDERTHALS WHO BOP THROUGH CLUTCHING GUITARS.
THAT'S NOT FAIR... SOME-TIMES IT'S SPECIAL... THAT GIRL IN AUSTRIA, SHE WAS INTELLIGENT... SHE WANTED TO MAKE ME BREAKFAST... WE'RE GONNA WRITE...
AND THAT DUTCH GIRL VISITED ME WHEN I WAS SICK... SHE NURSED ME BACK TO HEALTH ... SHE--
SHE THREW OVER HER STEADY BOY-FRIEND, WHICH SHOWS YA WHAT A CONFUSED LITTLE NUMBER SHE WAS...
CAN'T FOOL ME... YOU'RE INTO THE POWER-TRIP THING... I'VE SEEN ALL THAT SWEET YOUNG TAIL OBLIGE YOU, GOING ALL GAGA... I'VE SEEN YOU GETTING OFF ON GETTING THEM OFF...
I LOVE WALKING AROUND THE CLUB AFTER THE SHOW WITH A HUGE BONER.
J. SACCO 2.89

I'VE SEEN YOU ENTERING ROME IN TRIUMPH, GOOSE-STEPPING TO YOUR MENTAL TRUMPETS...
NOT ONLY DID I PULL THE TOTAL ROCK STAR THING AND BALL HER BACKSTAGE, BUT IN THE MORNING I STUMBLED TO THE COLOSSEUM AND HAD TWO CAPPUCINOS FOR 1600 LIRE.
YEAH, AND I'VE SEEN YOU SLOUCHING BEHIND AN AUSTRIAN BEER, DESPONDENT, REPENTENT...
IS THAT TOO MUCH TO ASK FOR?
A WIFE AND A DOGGIE?
AND I'VE HEARD VOICES CRACK WHEN THE TRUTH GURGLED OUT...
ALL I WANT IS A GIRL TO TALK TO...
I DON'T EVEN WANT TO SLEEP WITH HER...
JUST TALK...
IN ENGLISH.
FACE IT, YOU'RE FAR FROM HOME AND PARANOID ABOUT GETTING DICKED OVER... ALL THIS LONG-HAIRED, PSYCHEDELIC, LEATHER-CLAD, COCK-SCRATCHING POSTURING IS DIRECTLY PROPORTIONATE TO THOSE INSECURITIES TO YOUR LONELINESS, TO--
OKAY, OKAY, SIGMUND, WE GET LONELY... BIG DEAL... I SUPPOSE YOU DON'T?
I'M ALONG FOR THE SKETCHES, REMEMBER... I'M HERE AS AN OBSERVER, I'M--
FUCKIN', SO WHAT'RE THESE DOIN' IN YER POCKET?!!
HEY! GIMME THOSE BACK!!
J. SACCO 2-89

HMMMM... EROTIM... 'PRIMED FOR MAXIMUM SENSITIVITY WITH THE LUBRICATED--'
WHEN DID YOU PICK THOSE UP?
I DON'T REMEMBER.
LET ME GUESS... YOU DIDN'T BONE ONCE, THE WHOLE TOUR... NOT ONCE...
HUH?
I SAID, NO, DAMMIT!
WHAT A MORON.
ALL THE ONES I LIKED HAD BOYFRIENDS.
SO?
DIDN'T WE TELL YA?
YOU ASK, 'DO YOU HAVE A BOYFRIEND?'
AND IF THE ANSWER'S YES, YOU ASK--
'IS HE HERE?'
IT'S NOT SO EASY FOR ME!
WHY NOT?
I'M NOT SHAKING ASS ONSTAGE, I'M NOT A DUDED UP LEATHER-BOY... I'M SELLING YOUR FUCKING T-SHIRTS... THAT HARDLY QUALIFI ME AS A PRI-MARY SEXUAL ATTRACTI !!!
FUCKIN'...
YOU SUCK.
OKAY, OKAY...
I ADMIT IT...
I'M NO SWINGER...
AT FIRST, I KEPT MY COOL...
FIGURED SOMETHING WOULD COME MY WAY...
ROCK 'N' ROLL TOUR, MAN...
BOUND T'BE SEXUAL FALLOUT.
BUT NO ONE WAS LINING UP T'GET INTO MY PANTS...
DIDN'T HAVE T'TALK ANYONE OUT OF IT, LIKE GENE DID IN ROM
J SACCO 2·89

HOLD HIM DOWN... HE'S GETTING DELIRIOUS!
MEANWHILE, YOU GUYS WERE CENTAURS...
SCORING...
PICKING AND CHOOSING...
ROBERT NABBED THAT SWISS BIRD I WAS HOT FOR...
DIDN'T EVEN HAVE THE DECENCY T'BOFF...
ALL I WAS LEFT WITH WAS A FUCKING BURN MARK ON MY SKETCH-BOOK WHERE SHE HEATED HER HASH...
SEE?
Y'CAN STILL SEE IT!
THAT'S ENOUGH, JOE... YOU GOT SOME GREAT SKETCHES.
BUT THERE WERE OTHER SCARS...
BACKNANG...
REMEMBER THAT GIG?
THAT GIG WAS INSANE...
THE MUSIC...
AND THAT GIRL...
HER BOTTOM, IT WAS--
AND WE'RE PRESSED 'GAINST EACH OTHER...
SHE BENDS OVER...
I'M INSANE...
FIGURE IT'S AN INVITATION...
FIGURE I OUGHTA R.S.V.P.
SHIT! NOW HE'S GETTING ME HORNY!
NEXT THING I KNOW, I'M FALLING BACK, SLAMMING INTO A WALL, A NAIL GOUDGES A TWO-INCH GASH IN MY FOREARM...
THEN THERE WAS BERLIN...
SECOND TIME WE CAME THROUGH...
YOU WERE HILARIOUS IN BERLIN...
I WAS WASTED, TELLING EVERY-ONE I WAS GONNA SWING...
J. SACCO 2.89

BACKSTAGE BERLIN...
SPEED AVANTE GARDE MILLING ABOUT LIKE A HERD OF SUPERNOVAS
ARM CANDY RAILERS DISAPPEARING INTO THE CAN IN TWOS...
OH BOY, BERLIN
AND I'M GONNA SWING, DAMMIT...
BUT FIRST...
LET'S PARTY LIKE WE USED TO!
JA JA!
Rounds of TEQUILA
Swallowed smooth with orange slices
mmmmm.
cheers
who's this?
English doll, all kinds of artillery
fish 'n' chips
another round
we shall fight on the beaches
I'm bracketed
I'm caught in the barrage
I'm in smithereens
bit drinkers changing, but I'm the constant, the Star
ich bin ein Berliner!
it's LOVE...
wish she'd ditch the deutsche dude...
J. SACCO 2.89

uck it
downstairs
soaking
tequila
like we used to
tequila
set start
Gerry looking a bloated pastey Elvis
All too much
upstairs, lie down
room spin
passout
hunh? show over?
Gerry und someone
whole lotta love
Excuse me
Did you BLOW 'EM?
YEAH, I BLEW 'EM.
TOLDYA HE'D BLOW 'EM!
HIGH FIVE
J. SACCO 2.89

SLEEP OPTION DISCUSSION
REJECTION
BERLIN
GOTTA SWING
BERLIN
WHERE'D ARTILLERY GO?
PILING PILING PILING
INTO A CAR
DRIVER PULLS OVER
WANTS MATT
WANTS NOSE CANDY
PILING OUT
SURPRISE!
ARTILLERY!
DEUTSCHE IN TOW
SO, HOW'S ABOUT THAT ZANY EUROPEAN YOUTH MOVE-MENT?
THEN SHE FLOATS UP
SOMETHING TO SHOW
SHE SKETCHES, TOO
NOTHING MUCH
SKETCHES
SHAPE ON A BACKSTAGE BED
FACELESS
LYING FACELESS ON A BED
SCARE ME, THE SKETCHE
A PEN TURNED MY WAY
REMEMBER HER?
Schultheiss
Schultheiss
BACKSTAGE
FLIPPING THROUGH SKETCHBOOK
SPEED SWEETIE
Schultheiss
SLEEPS WEDNESDAYS
ARTILLERY YACKITY-YACK YACKING... WISH SHE'D SHUT UP... DON'T WANT TO VOMIT KEBAP ON HER...
J. SACCO 2.89

WASN'T TILL TWO DAYS LATER I REALIZED I'D LEFT SOMETHING BEHIND IN THAT BAR IN BERLIN THAT NIGHT...
THE 'MEMBER'S ONLY' WIND-BREAKER MY MOM GAVE ME...
THE ONE YOU GUYS USED T'TEASE ME ABOUT...
SO GUESS WHAT'S MY REACTION?
IT'S: GOOD, NOW I CAN GET ME A LEATHER JACKET.
HERE'S THE CLUB, BOYS.
WE'RE GONNA UNLOAD NOW...
HUTCH'LL DO MOST OF THE HEAVY WORK...
GERRY'S GOT A TWEEKED BACK...
HE'LL BUM CHANGE, FIND A PINBALL MACHINE.
GENE AND MATT MIGHT HELP HUTCH, MIGHT INVEST-IGATE BACK-STAGE...
COUNT THE BEERS.
ROBERT'LL SCAMPER OFF LIKE THE PUPPY HE IS...
COME BACK WITH A FULL REPORT.
CHECK IT OUT! THERE'S AN ALL-GIRL HIPPY BAND GONNA OPEN FOR US!!
ME?
I'M GONNA FIGURE OUT WHERE TO SET UP THE T-SHIRT CONCESSION...
Y'GOTTA THINK IN TERMS OF FOOT TRAFFIC...
T-shirts 20 PM M XL
J. SACCO 2·89

European tour poster. Or was it the Egyptian tour poster?

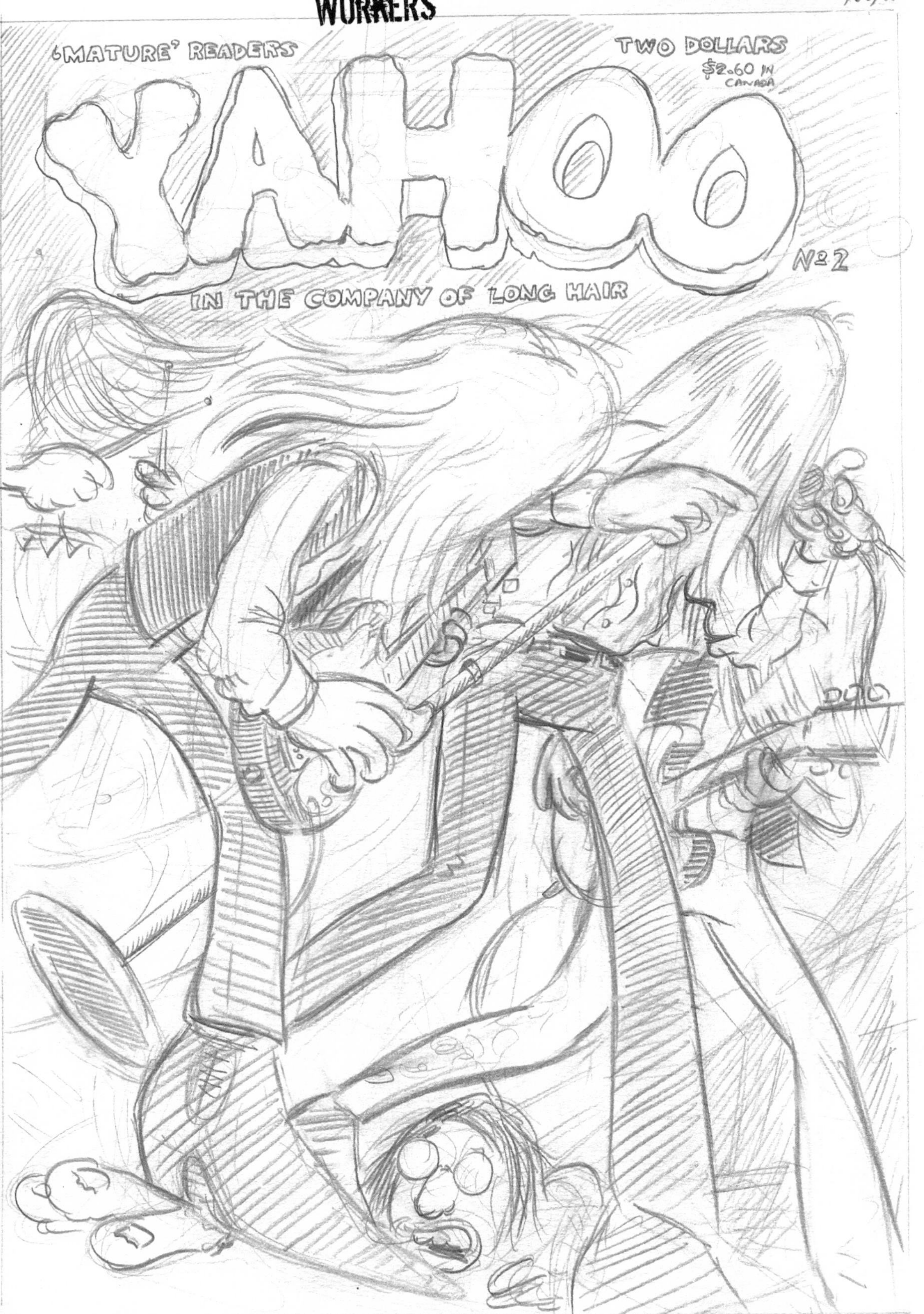

Pencil rough for the cover of Yahoo #2.
Note self-pitying self-portrait at the bottom.

Camille Lemmens, that magnificent Dutchman, was one of the Miracle Workers' drivers.

4/15/88
CARTOON ROB, ON THE WAY TO BERLIN
ZZZZZZZZZ
ROBERT BUTLER'S 115TH DREAM
HEY, GUYS. CHECK IT OUT.

4/16/88
GERRY, BERLIN, BEFORE THE HOSPITAL.
MATT, THE HANDSOME VERSION
BERLIN APT., WAITING FOR GERRY, WATCHING AN IGGY POP VIDEO
LICKY WORK FOR ME NOW. HE SUCK YOUR BALLS DRY.
ALL RIGHT, STOOGE ME.
HUTCH DRAWN WHILE DRUNK & STONED

Drawn from the wings during a performance.

5/4/88
ZZZZZ
GERRY TURNS ON THE CHARM AT BASSAGNO DEL GRAPPO.
HEY, GUYS! CHECK IT OUT!
KEEP YOUR EYES ON THE ROAD, ROGERS
HUH?
ITALIAN BUTT MAG ON THE WAY TO SPAIN
-ON THE FLAT TIRE IDEA.
GENNY: "ANY BAND THAT CAN'T PULL OFF THAT KIND OF SCAM ISN'T WORTH IT'S SALT."
GENE: "THAT'S GENIUS. HAVE SOME OF MY CHOCOLATE."
5/5/88
SO WHAT DO YOU THINK, GERRY? WHAT ARE THE FURTHER POTENTIALS FOR DISASTER?
MAKING DECISIONS IN SAN SEBASTIAN.
LET'S GO SWIMMING.
WAIT TILL MADRID
GENE TAKES CHARGE
RELAX, BOYS. WE'RE GOING TO MADRID.

MATT ON SAN SEBASTIAN:
"TOO MANY GIRLS IN THIS TOWN. NOT ENOUGH RECORD COLLECTORS WITH GLASSES AND POT BELLIES."
MITCH ON SPENDING BIG MONEY IN WARSAW: 5/5/88
"WE ATE, DRANK, BOUGHT TRUMPETS."
GERRY:
"LIFE DOES NOT EXIST IF YOU CAN'T WALK TO A 7-11."
GERRY EXPLAINS THE LAMENESS OF PORTLAND ON THE ROAD TO MADRID.
"I THINK I'M STARTING TO BURN OUT ON BURNING OUT." - MATT.
LURCH, ASLEEP, BUT NOT AT THE WHEEL, ON THE SPANISH PLAIN IN THE RAIN.
THE BAND LISTENS TO MATT'S SEXUAL EXPLOITS WITH HIS SISTER'S FRIENDS AS THEY WAIT FOR VALERIE'S CALL, MADRID.
GERRY: "SHE'S OUR MANAGER AND WE'RE MORONS."

"THE BOOKS ARE IN A MESS... NOT REALLY, BUT WE GOTTA GO OVER THE BOOKS WITH CAMILLE WHEN WE SEE HIM IN FOUR DAYS."
ON THE PHONE WITH RUDE
5/11/88
"ARE THE FUZZTONES GONNA HAVE A SHOW IN LONDON, TOO? ... HATE TO SPLIT UP THE POTENTIAL AUDIENCE... THAT'S COOL..."
FREE
NOW
MIRACLE WORKERS

5/11/88
LURCH LISTENING TO SOUNDCHECK, DORNBIRN
"THAT'S WHY DRUG USE COMES SO EASILY TO MUSICIANS. YOUR WHOLE LIFE IS CONDITIONED TO CRUISING UP AND DOWN. UP AND DOWN." - GERRY.
COME LIVE WITH ME IN L.A., SACCO, WE CAN BECOME GAY LOVERS, RECREATE WORLD WAR I BATTLES
GERRY

5/12/88
GERMAN BORDER
WRONG
POLIZEI
ZOLL
"SO. YOU LIKE MARIJUAN HASHISH?
COKE ME
I'M WAITING FOR THE DOGS.
ROB.
GERRY
HITCH
"I FEEL RAPED. MY ASS FEELS LOOSE. IT FELT SORT OF GOOD."

"I DIDN'T COME 10,000 MILES TO BE LEFT IN A HOTEL ROOM WHEN THERE'S FUN TO BE HAD. WRONG. WRONG. WRONG." - GERRY
"FUCK MELODY, IT JUST GETS IN THE WAY OF DISTORTION" - HUTCH.
5/19/88
PLEASANT IN ROTTERDAM.
ROB.
GERRY
STEPHEN
RUDE
ACCOUNTS, ROTTERDAM.

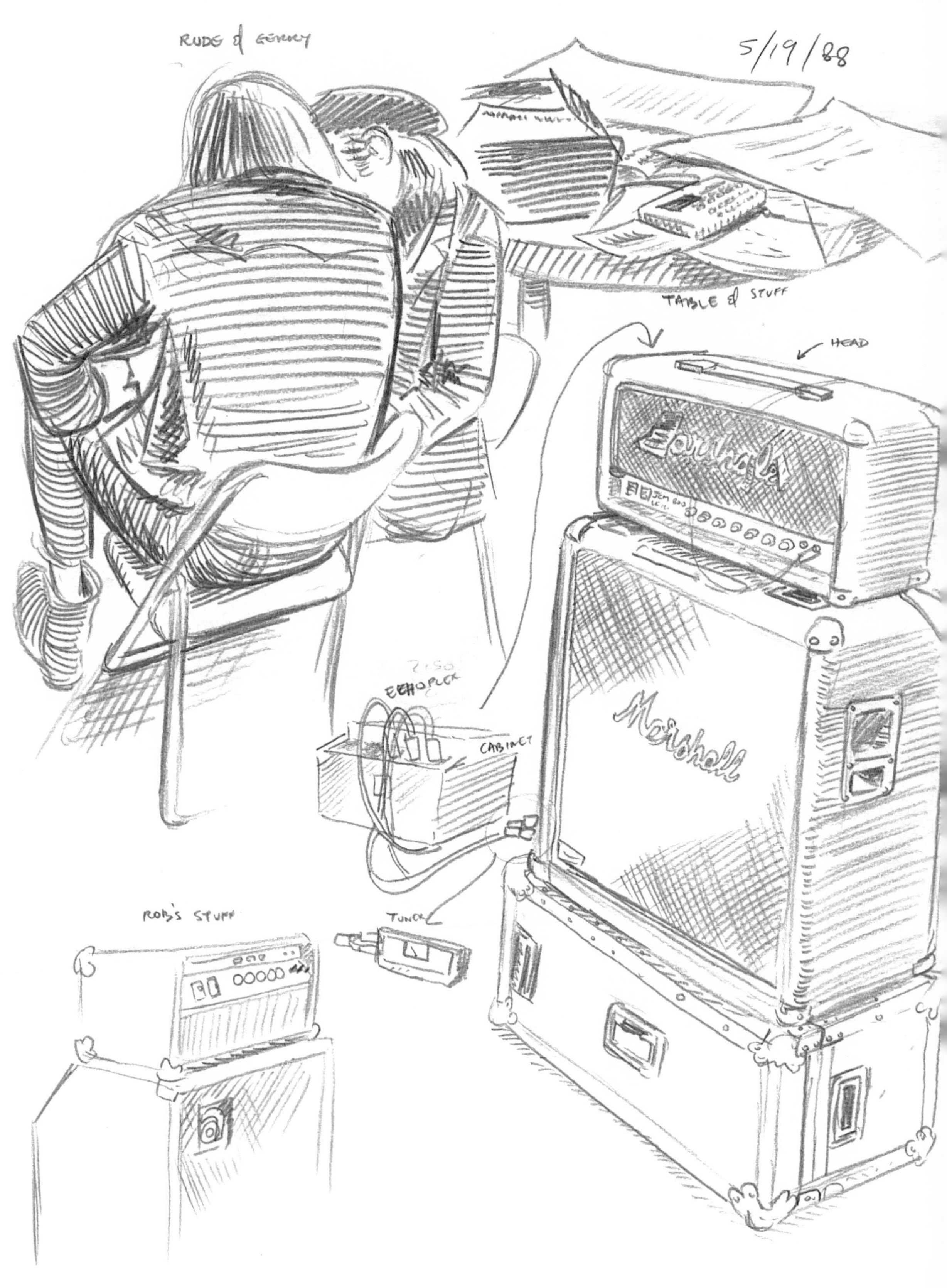
RUDE & GERRY
5/19/88
TABLE & STUFF
HEAD
Marshall
ECHOPLEX
CABINET
Marshall
ROB'S STUFF
TUNER

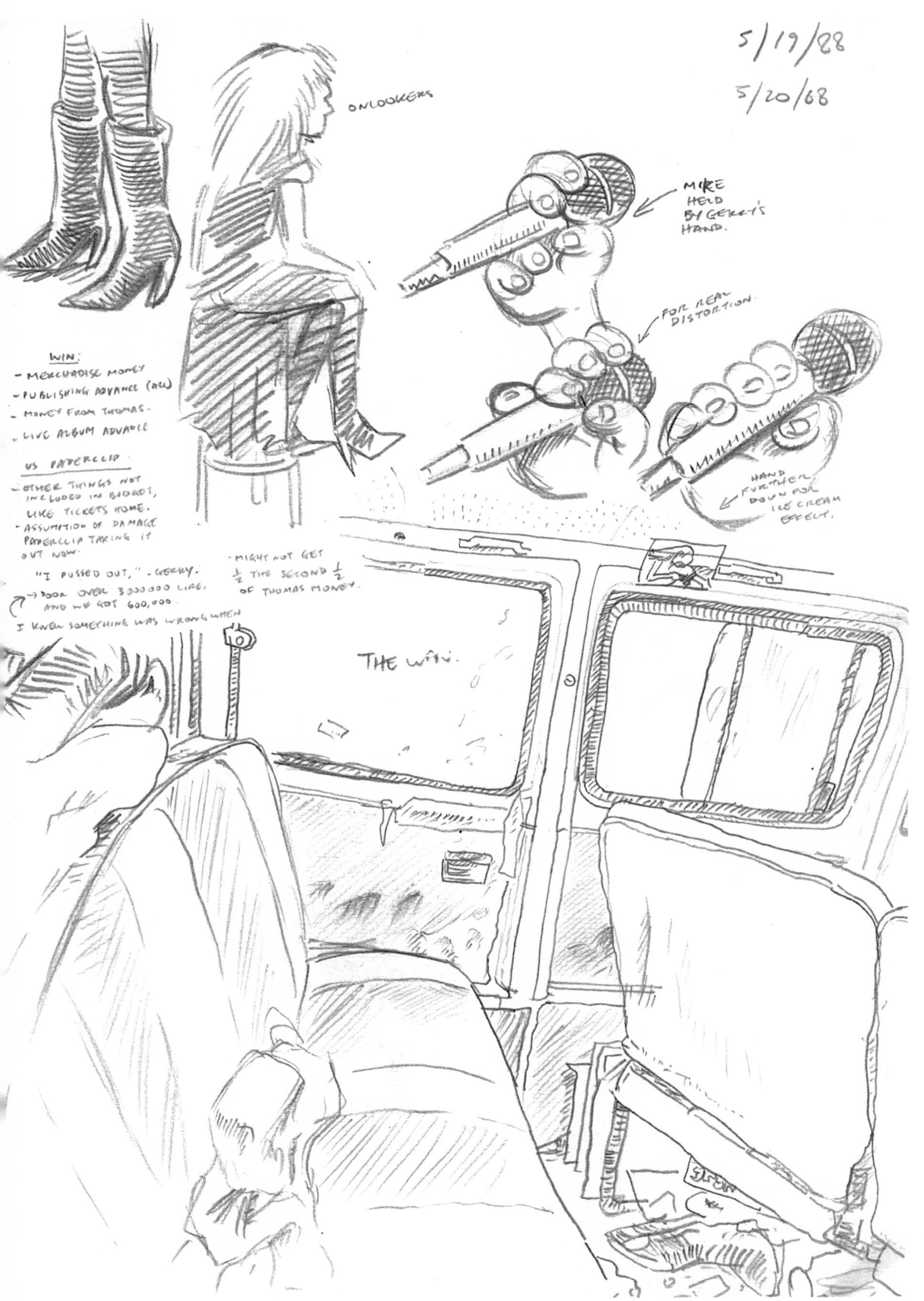
5/19/88
5/20/88
ONLOOKERS
MIKE HELD BY GERRY'S HAND.
FOR REAL DISTORTION.
HAND FURTHER DOWN FOR ICE CREAM EFFECT.
WIN:
- MERCHADISE MONEY
- PUBLISHING ADVANCE (ALL)
- MONEY FROM THOMAS -
- LIVE ALBUM ADVANCE
VS PAPERCLIP
- OTHER THINGS NOT INCLUDED IN BUDGET, LIKE TICKETS HOME.
- ASSUMPTION OF DAMAGE PAPERCLIP TAKING IT OUT NOW.
- MIGHT NOT GET ½ THE SECOND ½ OF THOMAS MONEY.
"I PUSSED OUT," - GERRY.
→ DOOR OVER 3000000 LIRE, AND WE GOT 600,000.
I KNEW SOMETHING WAS WRONG WHEN
THE VAN.

Character studies for Yahoo #2.

More character studies.

And more, still.

the TOP
by Joe Sacco © 1995
When Gerry moved up from L.A. to get off junk and assorted narcotics, I was expecting melodrama, spasms, an addict's half-mad pleadings for one last fix. I'd memorized my lines...
YER GONNA KICK THIS THING, GERRY... YER GONNA KICK IT IF IT KILLS YA!
HUH?

But if his cold turkey symptoms have proved a disappointment, there's no denying Gerry's hit rock bottom. He's got nothing. His rock career is a shambles. He says his girlfriend in L.A., also a junkie, ruined his life...
SHE LEFT ME 'CAUSE I WOULDN'T FUCK HER.
AND THAT ISN'T A GOOD REASON TO LEAVE YOU?
YOU DON'T HAVE A SEX DRIVE ON JUNK. SHE ONLY LIKED THE IDEA OF WANTING TO GET FUCKED.

Ugly? Yes, but Not-Exactly-Romeo-and-Juliet had their laughs. There was the time she came home late and delirious, and Gerry discovered rug burns on her back...
YOUR PRO-FESSOR?
BETWEEN THOSE PILLS YOU GOT AND THE ALCOHOL HE KEPT GIVING ME... I... WE...

Gerry got her to lure the professor over and...
YOU FUCKED MY GIRLFRIEND, MAN! I'M GONNA CALL THE POLICE AND SCHOOL AND CHARGE YOU WITH RAPE UNLESS YOU COME UP WITH SOME MONEY!
YOU'VE G-GOT TO G-GIVE ME A BREAK!
I AM GIVING YOU A BREAK!

HE WENT TO A BANK MACHINE AND CAME BACK WITH $300. WE TOOK IT. THEN WE CALLED UP SOME DEALER TO GET DOPE.

TO CELEBRATE.

Don't sneer, 'cause there's no way but up for Gerry, and psychodrama like he's seen can be an artist's ticket to the top. Psychodrama needs to stew a few years, that's all... it needs to be compressed under layers of fresher catastrophes, packed down and fossilized. One day Gerry will return for his psychodrama, he'll drill for it and it'll come up gushing, ready to be refined and turned into the fuel that drives his creative engine...

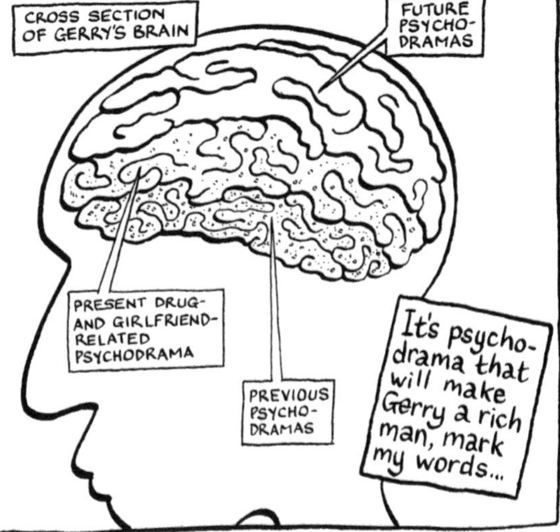

CROSS SECTION OF GERRY'S BRAIN

PRESENT DRUG- AND GIRLFRIEND-RELATED PSYCHODRAMA

It's psychodrama that will make Gerry a rich man, mark my words...

THE TOP

by Joe Sacco ©1995

I have this beautiful morning routine. I wake up, roll off my futon, and get right to work. Cartooning is a labor-intensive profession. You don't just shit out a comics masterpiece at half-time the Monday night before deadline...

ACHTUNG! MINES
DO NOT DISTURB

But when I wake up and find Gerry asleep on the couch, my beautiful morning routine is shattered. It's impossible to ignore Gerry on your couch and go about your day tra-la-la. Gerry is a disturbance who must be coaxed to his feet and lured out the door before he drops anchor for the day...

BREAKFAST? A SIDE OF POTATOES? I'LL BUY.

Don't get me wrong. I love Gerry and I'm grateful for his friendship...

LET'S TRY TO KEEP IT UNDER TWO BUCKS, OK?
NO SOUR CREAM.

...it's just that our different artistic disciplines require different sorts of efforts on our respective roads to the top.

For instance, Gerry will make it or break it in the public sphere, and you might not know it to look at him, but he's hard at work right now...

In the rock milieu, being seen is a stressful but necessary activity requiring an intimate knowledge of lighting, posture, and the fundamentals of indifference. And it is here, in cafes and bars, that Gerry will lock horns with the competition and serve notice that he is once again in the running for next Golden Boy...

Me? I've told you, I can't work with people around, so I'm skeptical when Gerry advances the idea of establishing a commune of artists in a rented warehouse. Everyone would have his or her own space, posits Gerry, but in the common room we'd all be jazzing off the collective energy, a New Renaissance would be inaugurated, artistic boundaries smashed, and bourgeois notions of sexuality dismissed...

Well and fine, but I want to know who'd do the dishes...

WE'D HAVE TO BE SERIOUS ABOUT THINGS LIKE THAT. THERE'S WAYS OF GETTING THINGS LIKE THAT DONE.

It's called fascism, of course, but I know Gerry could never make the trains run on time.

B SIDE: THE SWISS YEARS

MOST ALL OF THE FOLLOWING COMICS were written for a Swiss events magazine called *Agenda* and originally appeared in German. I wouldn't stand up in a court of law and testify that these are the best strips I ever drew. I was working on *Palestine* at the time, which, in its serialized form, was one of the poorest selling comics Fantagraphics ever published. I was broke. The *Agenda* gig was a god-send, and each of them paid almost as much as I was making for an entire 32-page issue of *Palestine*. (Christ, the Swiss have money to throw around.) But, eventually, setting aside the time to write and draw these strips every month really wore me down. I suppose they have their bitter charm. Kim Thompson suggested we publish all of them, arguing that a "Sacco completist" might want to have them. I don't think there is such a thing as a "Sacco completist," unless we're talking about my mother. Anyway, we threw out about a third of them, and I hope you're thankful. None of this rubbish has appeared in English before.

"Rock 'N' Roll Rot" and "Record Label Executive" were written for a Stateside smooth talker who convinced me he was about to launch a music magazine and that I would be his star artist. He never did launch anything AND he never paid me for these pieces, or maybe he did, but my outrage continues to this day, regardless. This is the first time they've seen the light of day in English.

SO YOU WANNA MEET A

Rock Star

I'M A FAIRLY IMPORTANT PERSON... A WELL KNOWN POSTER ARTIST IN BERLIN... AND NATURALLY, I'M INVITED BACKSTAGE AFTER EVERY SHOW...

WHICH WAY TO THE CHEESE PLATE?
RED CARPET

YOU, ON THE OTHER HAND, ARE PROBABLY NOT AS IMPORTANT... BUT DON'T DESPAIR... PERHAPS YOU, TOO, CAN GET A COVETED "ALL AREAS" ACCESS PASS AND EVENTUALLY MEET YOUR ROCK IDOLS... OF COURSE, IT HELPS TO MEET ONE OF THE FOLLOWING CONDITIONS...

YOU'RE A WELL-KNOWN POSTER ARTIST IN BERLIN.

SORRY, JUST WANTED TO DRAW MYSELF AGAIN.

YOU'RE THE GIRLFRIEND OF A WELL-KNOWN POSTER ARTIST IN BERLIN.

YOU KNOW THE PERSON PUTTING ON THE SHOW.

HE'S MY SON.

YOU ARE THE PERSON PUTTING ON THE SHOW.

I'M PUTTING MY MOM ON THE GUEST LIST.

LET'S FACE IT, IF YOU'RE NOT USEFUL TO THE BAND OR IF YOU'RE NOT SEXUALLY ATTRACTIVE, YOUR CHANCES OF MEETING THEM ARE MINIMAL.

THE ONLY OTHER HOPE YOU HAVE -- AND IT'S A SLIM ONE -- IS TO TRY TO CONVINCE A SYMPATHETIC ROADIE TO LET YOU INTO THE DRESSING ROOM AFTER THE SHOW TO GET A RECORD SIGNED...

HEY, THERE'S SOME GUY OUT HERE WHO WANTS TO GET HIS RECORD SIGNED.
Backstage
LED ZEPPELIN
IMPORTANT: MAKE SURE THE RECORD IS BY THE BAND YOU WANT TO MEET.

WHO KNOWS? IF LUCK IS WITH YOU, YOU MIGHT FIND YOURSELF SITTING RIGHT NEXT TO A ROCK STAR!

BORN TO PUKE

HEY, ANYONE KNOW WHERE WE'RE GOING TOMORROW?

ROCK 'N' ROLL ISN'T JUST A KIND OF BEAT MUSIC... IT'S A LIFESTYLE, AND LIKE ANY LIFESTYLE WORTH LIVING, IT SHOULD BE LIVED...

TO THE MAX

by Joe Sacco ©1991

JUST BEING PRESENT ISN'T ENOUGH... YOU HAVE TO BRING SOMETHING SPECIAL TO THE MIX... YOU HAVE TO BE A STEP AHEAD OF EVERYONE ELSE...

HER NOSE RING HAS A NOSE RING.
HER NOSE RING'S NOSE RING HAS A NOSE RING.

STAYING UP LATE ISN'T ENOUGH... ONE SHOULD NEVER GET TO SLEEP AT ALL...

HOW MANY HOURS DID YOU GET LAST NIGHT?

LAST NIGHT? I THOUGHT THAT TONIGHT WAS LAST NIGHT.

OF COURSE, MASTERING AN INSTRUMENT HELPS, BUT DESTROYING ONE IS FAR BETTER...

MY LES PAUL!
...ESPECIALLY IF IT'S NOT YOURS.

BUT BE ON YOUR GUARD! COMPETITION IS FIERCE. THERE'S ALWAYS SOMEONE READY TO LIVE MORE "TO THE MAX" THAN YOU...

PLEASE DO NOT FEED THE ROCKERS
MY BOY-FRIEND IS A JUNKIE!
OH YEAH? WELL, MY BOY-FRIEND IS A DEAD JUNKIE!

J. SACCO 8-91

DEATH of a ROADIE

by Joe Sacco

EVER SINCE HE WAS A CHILD, RUDOLPH HAD A DREAM.
MY ONLY DESIRE IS TO CARRY AROUND HEAVY EQUIPMENT FOR A ROCK BAND.

FINALLY HIS DREAM CAME TRUE...
WATCH OUT!
MOM

WHAT HAPPENED TO HIM?
I THINK HE GOT HURT.
DOES THIS MEAN I'VE GOT TO CARRY MY OWN GUITAR?

OF COURSE, A GOOD ROADIE LIKE RUDOLPH KNOWS THAT THE SHOW MUST GO ON.
BUT YOU'LL BE LATE FOR THE SHOW IF YOU TAKE ME TO THE HOSPITAL.
HOSPITAL? WE'RE TAKING YOU TO THE CHEWING GUM FACTORY.

WHAT A RIP OFF! WE GOT TWICE AS MUCH FOR THE LAST ROADIE.
CHEWHOUSE GUM AND CO.
RAW MATERIAL ENTRANCE.

BUT RUDOLPH'S MEMORY REMAINS IN THE BAND MEMBERS' HEARTS.
AFTER THE CONCERT.
AND I SAID, "WATCH OUT!" BUT IT WAS ALREADY TOO LATE.
IT'S HORRIBLE!
YES. AND I DON'T THINK I CAN SLEEP ALONE TONIGHT...

J. SACCO 9-91

The ROCK JOURNALIST

by Joe Sacco © 1991

CAN YOU PICK OUT THE ROCK JOURNALIST?

WHERE'S THE BEER?
WHERE'S THE AFTERSHOW PARTY?
DO I GET A FREE T-SHIRT?
DOES ANYONE HAVE ANY COMMENT?
PRESS

YEP! HE'S THE ONE ASKING THE IMPORTANT QUESTIONS.

AND HE NEVER FAILS TO COME UP WITH THE IMPORTANT ANSWERS.

I'D SAY YOUR NEW SINGLE SOUNDS LIKE A FUSION OF THE MUSIC OF THE LAST THREE CENTURIES -- LIKE MOZART PLAYING FEED-BACK AT AN EDITH PIAF CONCERT WHILE SHE AMPUTATES BOB DYLAN'S LEGS.

HUH? WHAT? I'M A BIT DEAF.

DAY AND NIGHT HE STRUGGLES UNDER THE WEIGHT OF HIS ARTI-CLES, SEARCHING FOR PRECISELY THE RIGHT WORDS UNTIL, FINALLY, INSPIRATION ARRIVES.

AH! GREAT! THE BRITISH ROCK PRESS! LET'S SEE WHAT THEY'VE WRITTEN!

WHEN HE'S NOT BEHIND HIS DESK YOU'LL FIND THE ROCK JOURNALIST IN RECORD STORES. IS HE LOOKING FOR OBSCURE ALBUMS IN ORDER TO EXPAND HIS MUSICAL HORIZONS?

I'LL GIVE YOU TWO BUCKS FOR IT.
ONLY TWO? THAT RECORD IS IN MINT CONDITION! I DIDN'T PLAY IT ONCE!
HEAVY METAL
HEAVIER METAL
HEAVIEST METAL

NO! HE'S SELLING THE PROMO-TIONAL RECORDS HE RECEIVES EVERY DAY IN THE MAIL.

AND WHEN HIS ARTICLE IS PUBLISHED?

HEY, I DIDN'T SAY THIS STUFF ABOUT MOZART!
MOZART? NEVER HEARD OF THEM.
AHEM, I'VE GOT TO BE LEAVING! I'VE GOT ANOTHER INTERVIEW IN HALF AN HOUR!

J. SACCO 10-91

I DON'T KNOW IF YOU FEEL THE SAME WAY, BUT I'D RATHER SHOOT MYSELF THAN WATCH THOSE AWFUL, WRETCHED THINGS ABOUT THAT SHINY, MAKE-BELIEVE WORLD... THE WORLD OF THE DAMNED...

MUSIC VIDEOS

by Joe Sacco ©1992

IT'S A SOURCE OF ENDLESS WONDER TO ME HOW PEOPLE CAN SIT FOR HOURS WATCHING THEM.

THE WORST THING ABOUT MUSIC VIDEOS IS THAT THEY ALLOW "STARS" WITH EXTREMELY QUESTIONABLE MUSICAL SKILLS THE CHANCE TO EXHIBIT THEIR EVEN MORE QUESTIONABLE ACTING ABILITIES.

OH! DID YOU SEE HOW HE BRUSHED HIS HAIR AWAY FROM HIS FACE?
I'M SENDING IN AN OSCAR NOMINATION.

EVERYTHING ABOUT MUSIC VIDEOS IS PREDICTABLE. GIRLS IN SHORT SKIRTS ALWAYS MEET UP WITH BOYS IN TIGHT TROUSERS AND GIRLS IN EVEN TIGHTER TROUSERS.

GOD, IT'S SO ROMANTIC!

THAT'S WHAT I THOUGHT ABOUT THIS BOTTLE OF CHAMPAGNE, WHICH I PICKED UP ESPECIALLY FOR THIS OCCASION.

WHAT'S THAT, DARLING?

THOSE SUPERQUICK CUTS, THOSE HECTIC SET AND COSTUME CHANGES — THEY'RE ENOUGH TO MAKE ONE PUKE.

IS THERE ANY POPCORN LEFT?
AHEM...
HURL

WHAT I'D REALLY ENJOY SEEING, FOR ONCE, IS VIDEOS ABOUT TRULY TALENTED AND EXPRESSIVE PEOPLE. FOR EXAMPLE, CARTOONISTS LIKE ME...

SO, SHOULD I PUT IN MY DIAPHRAGM NOW, HONEY-BUNNY?
NOT JUST YET! THIS IS THE PART WHERE I RULE A COUPLE DOZEN STRAIGHT LINES WHILE SENSITIVELY BRUSHING THE HAIR FROM MY EYES.

J. SACCO 12-91

SHE CAME OUT OF NOWHERE AND SUDDENLY SHE WAS EVERYWHERE! HER FACE WAS ON THE COVER OF EVERY ROCK MAGAZINE! EVERYONE TALKED ABOUT HER! EVERYONE WANTED TO KNOW EVERYTHING ABOUT HER, EVEN HER SHOE SIZE. DON'T ASK ME WHY. I THINK SHE'S...

a teenage bore

by Joe Sacco ©1992

THE TEENAGE BORE HAS A LOT OF INTERESTING THINGS TO SAY.

TRUE LOVE DOESN'T EXIST.
SUICIDE IS THE ONLY WAY OUT.
MAKE-UP IS REALLY EXPENSIVE.
BRAVO!
SUCH DEPTH!
AMAZING INSIGHTS!

WHAT MAKES THE DECLARATIONS OF THE TEENAGE BORE SO PIERCING?

SHE IS THE VOICE OF A FRUSTRATED, MISUNDERSTOOD GENERATION OF YOUNG PEOPLE WHO LIVE SEEMINGLY POINTLESS LIVES IN SUBURBAN NOTHINGNESS -- BUT WHO GET ENOUGH POCKET MONEY TO SHIFT MEGA-UNITS IN RECORD STORES.
MY MOTHER'S PARACHUTE DIDN'T OPEN
AN EXPERT

HER MINIONS HANDLE HER WITH KID GLOVES. THEY SUGAR-COAT BAD NEWS. NO ONE DARES CROSS HER!

SHE'S DEMANDED WE CLOSE DOWN THE CLUB AND THROW THE OWNER'S WIFE AND KIDS INTO A TANK OF PIRANHAS!
WHERE ARE WE GONNA FIND PIRANHAS IN THE MIDDLE OF THE NIGHT?
THERE'S A PLANE LEAVING FOR THE AMAZON IN ONE HOUR!

BUT JUST AS RAPIDLY AS HER STAR ROSE, HER STAR FALLS UNDER THE GUNS OF THE CRITICS.

TRUE LOVE DOESN'T EXIST.
SUICIDE IS THE ONLY WAY OUT.
MAKE-UP ISN'T SO EXPENSIVE NOW THAT I'VE MADE A BUNCH OF MONEY.
SHE'S LOST HER EDGE!
WHERE'S HER SHARP WIT?

AND NOW IT'S ALL OVER; HER CAREER HAS COME TO AN ABRUPT END. HER ONLY CHANCE NOW IS TO WAIT 20 YEARS AND ATTEMPT A COMEBACK.

TRUE LOVE DOESN'T EXIST.
SUICIDE IS THE ONLY WAY OUT.
PLASTIC SURGERY IS REALLY EXPENSIVE.

BUT WHO'S GOING TO SING THE PRAISES OF A MIDDLE-AGED BORE?

J. SACCO 12·91

THE CONCERT DOESN'T START FOR A FEW HOURS YET, BUT THERE'S ALREADY A MASS OF PEOPLE IN THE STADIUM. AUDIENCE MEMBERS? NO! IT'S THE ARMY OF CONSTRUCTION WORKERS AND ROADIES BUILDING THE STAGE FOR THE LATEST...

ROCK SPECTACLE!

by JOE SACCO ©1992

AND HERE'S THE STAGE! RUINS FLOWN IN FROM ROME! PYRAMIDS SHIPPED IN FROM EGYPT! RAIN FOREST TRUCKED UP FROM BRAZIL! BUT NOW THERE'S A LITTLE PROBLEM!

WE DON'T HAVE ROOM FOR THE SPEAKERS!

NO PROBLEM! THE AUDIENCE WILL GO INSANE ANYWAY ONCE THE SHOW STARTS. THEY'LL REDUCE THE STADIUM TO RUBBLE, BURN THE STAGE TO ASH AND CINDERS, AND SLAUGHTER THE MUSICIANS... AND THAT'S DURING THE OPENING ACT!

HERE COMES THE HEADLINER! THEY'RE PLAYING FROM A DIRIGIBLE OVER THE STADIUM. THE DIRIGIBLE FLIES ON TO THE NEXT STADIUM! AND THE NEXT!

BUT WILL THE SPECTACLE SATISFY THE CROWD?

I HEARD THEY'RE GOING TO END THE SHOW WITH A NUCLEAR EXPLOSION.
AGAIN?! THEY ALWAYS END THEIR SHOW WITH A NUCLEAR EXPLOSION.
J. SACCO '5.92

ELEVATOR TO HELL

by Joe Sacco ©1992

THIS IS REVEREND BLESSBUNNY. HE THINKS POP MUSIC IS UNDERMINING THE MORALITY OF THE NATION'S YOUTH.
THESE LYRICS! LOATHSOME! NOT EVEN IN MY MOST TWISTED FANTASIES COULD I IMAGINE DOING THAT TO A FARM ANIMAL!
2 LIVE CRUDE
NOT IF IT COULD IDENTIFY ME IN A POLICE LINE-UP, ANYWAY.

HE PREACHES HIS MESSAGE AS OFTEN AS HE CAN AND WHEREVER POSSIBLE.
WHOEVER LISTENS TO THESE RECORDS WILL BE GOING STRAIGHT TO HELL!
TO HELL? SOUNDS GREAT!

BUT INSTEAD OF DISSUADING PEOPLE FROM SUCH RECORDS, HIS EFFORTS ACHIEVE THE OPPOSITE: THEY BECOME EVEN MORE CURIOUS.
WOW, THAT PADRE KNOWS WHAT HE'S TALKING ABOUT! WHEN I PLAY THIS RECORD BACKWARDS, IT COMMANDS US TO SHOOT OURSELVES IN THE HEAD!
I'LL GO LOAD THE SHOTGUN!

AND SO HELL GREETS A COUPLE OF NEWCOMERS.
HERE'S YET ANOTHER TWO ROCK FANS, YOUR SATANICNESS.
MORE ROCK FANS? IT'S GETTING TOO CROWDED DOWN HERE!
COOL.

SATAN DECIDES TO PAY A VISIT TO THE HONORABLE REVEREND.
HEY, HELL IS BOOKED UP FOR THE SUMMER? NO MORE ROCK FANS, OKAY? WE'VE GOT A FIRE CODE TO CONSIDER.
OH, ER, I UNDERSTAND.

WILL THIS BE THE END OF REVEREND BLESSBUNNY'S CAMPAIGN?
WHOEVER READS THESE BOOKS WILL GO STRAIGHT TO HELL!
THAT GUY'S DRIVING ME NUTS!

J. SACCO 6·92

DESTROYING A HOTEL ROOM IS NOT SIMPLY A MATTER OF KICKING IN THE DOOR, THROWING THE FURNITURE OUT THE WINDOW, AND VOMITING UNDER THE BED. IF YOU'RE A MUSICIAN WITH A REPUTATION AS A HELL-RAISER, YOU KNOW HOW IMPORTANT IT IS TO SMASH UP THE PLACE AS THOROUGHLY AS POSSIBLE. WHO CAN HELP YOU WITH THAT? US, THAT'S WHO! WE'RE...

THE HOTEL ROOM DESTRUCTION SPECIALISTS

by Joe Sacco ©1992

EFFECTIVE, FRIENDLY SERVICE AT AFFORDABLE RATES!

YOU WON'T HAVE TO LIFT A FINGER! WHILE YOU RECOVER FROM AN EXHAUSTING CONCERT, WE SMASH EVERYTHING TO BITS WITH THE MOST UP-TO-DATE HOTEL FURNITURE PULVERIZING MACHINERY.

AND DON'T WORRY! WE WON'T TOUCH THE TELEVISION TILL THE VERY LAST MOMENT!

IN THE SECOND ROUND, WE BRING IN OUR HAND GRENADE AND FLAMETHROWER UNIT TO GIVE YOUR ROOM THE MUCH-DESIRED "RUBBLE AND ASHES" LOOK!

YOU WILL BE DELIGHTED BY OUR SPECIAL TOUCHES AND THE RANGE OF OUR INEXPENSIVE EXTRAS -- FOR EXAMPLE, THE DEAD GOATS IN THE SHOWER AND AN ASSORTMENT OF OBSCENITIES DAUBED ONTO THE WALLS IN PIGS' BLOOD.

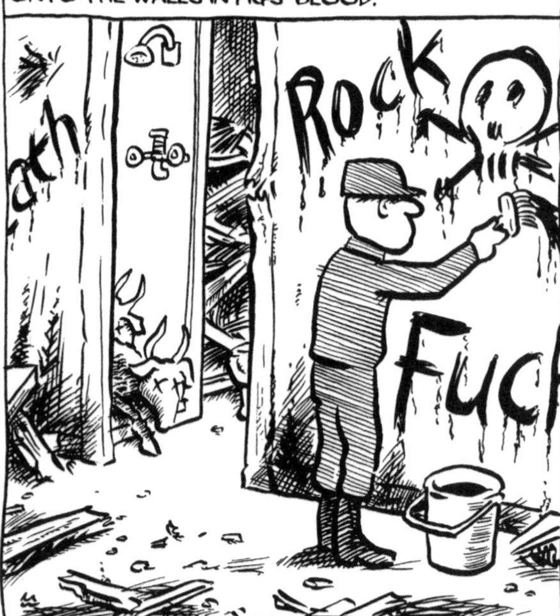

WHEN THE TIME COMES AND THAT VERY SPECIAL GROUPIE CROSSES THE THRESHOLD OF WHAT USED TO BE YOUR HOTEL ROOM, SHE WON'T HAVE THE SLIGHEST DOUBT THAT YOU ARE A GENUINE ROCK'N'ROLL "WILD MAN"!

J. SACCO 6.92

The Guitars of the Stars

by Joe Sacco ©1992

MORE AND MORE FREQUENTLY THESE DAYS ROCK MUSICIANS ARE USING SPECIAL INSTRUMENTS TO MATCH THEIR PERSONAL NEEDS...

HERE WE HAVE A GUITAR THAT HAS BEEN BUILT DIRECTLY INTO THE SPEAKER FOR A MUSICIAN WHOSE TRADEMARK IS ENDLESS FEEDBACK.

THIS PRE-SMASHED GUITAR WAS ORDERED BY AN AGING PUNK ROCKER WHO IS NO LONGER CAPABLE OF SWINGING A GUITAR OVER HIS HEAD AND SMASHING IT ON THE STAGE HIMSELF. HE CAN JUST SCATTER THESE PIECES ACROSS THE STAGE WHILE THOUSANDS CHEER.

THIS EDIBLE GUITAR WAS SPECIALLY DESIGNED FOR A MUSICIAN WHO THINKS HENDRIX DIDN'T TAKE THINGS FAR ENOUGH. NOT ONLY WILL HE BURN HIS GUITAR ON STAGE... HE'LL EAT IT AS WELL. BUT NOT RAW.

AND YOU? WHAT KIND OF GUITAR CAN I SELL YOU?

THAT ONE THERE WITH THE SIX STRINGS.

OH, Y'GOTTA BE DIFFERENT, DO YA?

J. SACCO 7.92

THE THEORY OF THE MONTH: YOU CAN JUDGE A BAND'S SUCCESS BY ITS...

TRANSPORTATION

by Joe Sacco ©1992

LET'S CONSIDER THE CAREER OF BAND X. ON THEIR FIRST TOUR, THEY'RE COMPLETELY UNKNOWN. NO ONE HAS EVER HEARD OF THEM, NOT EVEN THEIR TOUR MANAGER.
WE'LL NEVER GET TO THE CONCERT BY AUGUST!
NEXT TIME WE'LL GET A ROADIE WITH TWO LEGS!

BAND X'S GREAT BREAK-THROUGH IS SLOW IN COMING, DESPITE RISING ATTENDANCE FIGURES AND GOOD REVIEWS.
NEXT TIME WE'LL GET A BUS WITH AN ENGINE!
OH, SHUT UP!

AFTER THEY'VE HAD A HIT SINGLE, THEIR TRANSPOR-TATION PROS-PECTS CHANGE DRAMATICALLY.
AND THAT'S THE BUS OF THE SOUND ENGINEER.

BUT IT'S NOT UNTIL BAND X ARE AN INTERNATIONAL PHENOMENON THAT THEY BEGIN TO ENJOY THE ULTIMATE TRANSPORTATION OPTIONS...
IS THAT BAND X ON ITS WAY TO PARIS?
NOPE! THAT'S PARIS ON ITS WAY TO BAND X!

J. SACCO 9.92

TODAY WE ARE DEALING WITH A VERY SPECIAL SPECIES OF MUSIC LOVER, THE KIND WHO IS NEVER SATISFIED, WHO IS NEVER HAPPY TILL HE HAS IT ALL. WE'RE TALKING ABOUT...

The Record Collector

by Joe Sacco

© 1992

THIS NUT HERE, FOR EXAMPLE, WANTS TO OWN EVERY PICTURE DISC EVER MANUFACTURED.

LET'S LISTEN TO ONE OF THESE.
ARE YOU INSANE? YOU CAN'T JUST TAKE IT OUT OF ITS SLEEVE! NOT IN THIS LIGHT! THAT'S TOTALLY OUT OF THE QUESTION!
BESIDES, I DON'T HAVE A RECORD PLAYER.

THEN THERE ARE THE FREAKS WHO ARE ARE ALWAYS ON THE PROWL FOR "OUTTAKES," "ALTERNATIVE TRACKS," AND OTHER OBSCURITIES BY THEIR FAVORITE BANDS.

WOW! A FOUR-CD NIRVANA SET COMPRISING THE NOISES THEIR GUITAR CASES MAKE WHEN BEING OPENED AND CLOSED!

DO THEY HAVE THAT AS A PICTURE DISC?

ONE CAN ONLY PITY THE POOR COLLECTOR WHO FINALLY REALIZES HIS COLLECTION WILL PROBABLY NEVER BE COMPLETE.

HE LEARNED THAT ALL THE FIRST UGANDAN PRESSINGS OF THE HUMAN LEAGUE PICTURE DISC WERE STOLEN BY TANZANIAN REBELS WHO MELTED THEM DOWN TO MAKE AUTOMOBILE SEAT COVERS.

EVENTUALLY THE COLLECTOR LOSES ALL SENSE OF PROPORTION. WILL HE EVER KNOW WHEN TO STOP?

THIS IS MY NEWEST ACQUISITION. NOW I'VE ALMOST GOT A COMPLETE COLLECTION OF SEATTLE GRUNGE BANDS FROM THE LATE '80S.

HEY, WHEN DO WE EAT?

GRUNGE

MUDBUNNY

J. SACCO 10.92

ARE YOU AND YOUR PALS '60S FANATICS? THE TYPE THAT CAN'T GET ENOUGH PAISLEY? WELL, NOW YOU CAN OFFER YOUR FRIENDS SOMETHING SPECIAL -- A PARTY THEY'LL NEVER FORGET. THROW YOUR OWN...

INDOOR WOODSTOCK!

by Joe Sacco ©1993

THE PREPARATIONS: PUMP MUD INTO THE LIVING ROOM. ADD BROKEN BOTTLES AND PLASTIC CUPS. THEN LET THE NEIGHBORHOOD DOGS IN TO ADD THEIR OWN "SPECIAL" CONTRIBUTION.

PORTABLE POTTY
INSTALL A PORTA-POTTY.
PUT THE STEREO IN A BACK ROOM TO ACHIEVE THAT MUFFLED "FESTIVAL SOUND."

NOW THE GUESTS CAN BE LET IN. ENCOURAGE THEM TO STRIP IMMEDIATELY AND WALLOW IN THE DIRT TO RECREATE THE ATMOSPHERE OF WILD ABANDON AND "TOGETHERNESS" SO PERFECTED BY THE HIPPIES.

AT REGULAR INTERVALS, WORK THE PARTY-GOERS OVER WITH A GARDEN HOSE TO SIMULATE THE UNAVOIDABLE RAIN SHOWERS THAT OCCUR DURING OUTDOOR EVENTS.

OF COURSE, MAKE SURE THE TOILETS ARE LOCKED.

FINALLY, CALL UP THE POLICE AND COMPLAIN ABOUT A LOUD, WILD PARTY FULL OF OBNOXIOUS, FILTHY PEOPLE. GIVE THEM YOUR ADDRESS. AS THE POLICE BUST DOWN THE DOOR AND BEAT THEM TO A PULP, YOUR GUESTS WILL SAVOR THAT "US-VS-THEM" ATTITUDE THAT SO CHARACTERIZED THE '60S YOUTH MOVEMENT.

THANKS A LOT! LET'S DO IT AGAIN SOON!

J. SACCO 1-93

ROCKIN' SENIORS

by Joe Sacco ©1993

SOME BANDS HAVE BEEN AROUND FOR SO LONG THAT NO ONE CAN REMEMBER A TIME WHEN THEY DIDN'T EXIST.

STOP THE OFFENSIVE!
I JUST GOT FRONT ROW TICKETS TO THE ROLLING STONES!

THEY USED TO BE YOUNG, SNOTTY MUSICIANS WHO BELIEVED THEY'D BE 21 FOREVER.

I AIN'T GONNA BE IN A ROCK BAND WHEN I'M 30. PEOPLE OVER 30 ARE LAME. THEY OUGHT TO BE SHOT.

OF COURSE THEY ALL END UP PLAYING A DIFFERENT TUNE.

WOULD I STILL PLAY AT THE AGE OF 60? WELL, OF COURSE! IT DOESN'T MATTER HOW OLD YOU ARE. IT'S HOW YOUNG YOU FEEL!

AHH, HAS ANYONE SEEN MY HEMORRHOID CREAM?

MEANWHILE THEIR WIVES AND GIRLFRIENDS GROW EVER YOUNGER.

WILL YOU CLIMB OFF THAT STUPID ROCKING HORSE AND HELP ME FIND MY NOSE HAIR CLIPPERS?

BUT THE MOST IMPORTANT QUESTION IS, WHEN WILL THEY FINALLY STOP PLAYING?

I WROTE THIS NEXT SONG IN THE MIDDLE OF THE LAST CENTURY. WE'LL START AS SOON AS KEITH HAS FINISHED HIS PORRIDGE.

GOOD BOY.

J. SACCO 6·93

HE'S SENSITIVE, HE'S CONSIDERATE, HE LOVES EVERYTHING AND EVERYONE, HE WOULDN'T HURT A FLY. HE IS...

THE MUSICIAN WITH A MISSION

by Joe Sacco © 1993

ALL THE WARS, THE HORRIBLE BATTLES, AND THE GREAT CONFLICTS WOULD COME TO AN END IF ONLY WE WOULD ALL HOLD HANDS AND...
AHH...
AND BUY MY LATEST CD, WHICH IS BEING RELEASED NEXT WEEK.
I ♡ WHALES
I ♡ THE OZONE
SARAJEVO

HE SEEMS TO BE EVERYWHERE AT ONCE, ALWAYS AT THE RIGHT PLACE AT THE RIGHT TIME. HE'S GOT A SMOOTHLY WORKING TEAM TO ORGANIZE HIS ENDLESS BENEFIT SHOWS...

AND AFTER THE CONCERT IN BOMBAY FOR HOMELESS LEPERS YOU'VE GOT A PRESS CONFERENCE IN NEW YORK TO ANNOUNCE THE PUBLICATION OF YOUR BOOK, "HOW I SOLVED THE BOSNIAN CRISIS."

I WROTE A BOOK?

WELL, YES. IT'S GOING TO BE A SURPRISE TO EVERYONE.

I ♡ STARVING BABIES

I ♡ ♡

BUT AFTER A FEW YEARS HE SLOWLY RUNS OUT OF IDEAS FOR SOCIALLY CONSCIOUS SONGS.
MY FIRST RECORD WAS ABOUT THE ETHIOPIAN FAMINE. THEN I TACKLED THE RAIN FOREST ISSUE AND THE PROBLEMS OF THE INNER CITY. MY NEW BOX SET IS ABOUT THE PRICE OF MILK.
UDDERLY TOO HIGH

INTERESTINGLY, NONE OF THE WORLD'S PROBLEMS GET SOLVED DESPITE HIS BEST EFFORTS.
YOUR MORNING PAPER, SIR.
MY GOD, THEY'VE DROPPED A NUCLEAR BOMB ON PAKISTAN.
I SUPPOSE THAT'S MY NEXT SINGLE.

J. SACCO 6.93

Who Sleeps with Whom in the Music Business
by Joe Sacco ©1993

BLUES SINGER
HIS BEST FRIEND'S WIFE.
IF Y'LOSE YER WOMAN, PRAY GOD Y'DON'T LOSE YER MIND...

COUNTRY SINGER
HIS BEST FRIEND'S EX-WIFE.
THERE'S A TEAR IN MY BEER 'CAUSE I'M CRYIN' FOR YOU, DEAR...
XXX

GLAM ROCKER
HIS BEST FRIEND.
I WAS MADE FOR LOVIN' YOU...

DOOM ROCKER
HIS BEST FRIEND'S DEAD GIRLFRIEND.
ALL WE ARE SAYING, IS GIVE DOOM A CHANCE...

PUNK ROCKER
HIS BEST FRIEND'S GOAT.
I DON'T WANT A BABY THAT LOOKS LIKE THAT...
J. SACCO 8·93

NO TRAIN STATION IS SAFE FROM THEM. THEY LINE THE WALLS OF EVERY URINE-SOAKED PEDESTRIAN PASSAGE. IS THERE A STREET CORNER WITHOUT ONE? THEY FLAIL AWAY AT THEIR GUITARS AND LET OUT AN UNEARTHLY MOAN. RUN FOR IT! IT'S ANOTHER...

SINGER-SONGWRITER

by Joe Sacco ©1993

THE AVERAGE SINGER-SONGWRITER IS HIGHLY SENSITIVE AND KNOWS TRUE SUFFERING.
OH, MAN, I'M IN PAIN ♫
OH, MAN, AND IT LOOKS LIKE RAIN ♫

YOU, TOO, SHALL KNOW TRUE SUFFERING - JUST BY LISTENING TO HIM.

HE SINGS FOR SPARE CHANGE. HIS HAT IS HIS BANK. WHEN YOU DON'T DEPOSIT ENOUGH, HE JUST KEEPS ON SINGING. AND SINGING AND SINGING AND SINGING.

HERE! HERE'S MY WALLET! MY WATCH! PLEASE, PLEASE STOP!

STRANGELY, DESPITE HIS ANGST-RIDDEN BEARING -- OR BECAUSE OF IT -- HE'S ALWAYS A HIT WITH THE LADIES.

HOW DO YOU STAND YOUR PAIN?

INDEED. AND WHO KNOWS WHERE MY NEXT TENDER-LOIN IS COM-ING FROM?

PLEASE LET ME COOK FOR YOU!

DO NOT ALLOW ONE OF THESE FELLOWS INTO YOUR HOME. YOU MIGHT NEVER GET RID OF HIM.
I'LL BE APPEARING IN THE KITCHEN IN 20 MINUTES. SMALL DONATIONS WILL BE BE GRATEFULLY ACCEPTED.
J. SACCO 9.93

Rock 'n' Roll Romance

by Joe Sacco © 1994

SHE STANDS OUTSIDE THE CLUB WAITING FOR HER IDOL. IF SHE COULD ONLY CATCH HIS EYE FOR A SPLIT SECOND, SHE WOULD BE HAPPY FOR THE REST OF HER LIFE.
TONIGHT: MAX ZERO IN CONCERT
HEY YOU! MAX ZERO WANTS FEMALE COMPANY FOR THE NIGHT! INTERESTED?
ROAD CREW
INTERESTED? WHO WOULDN'T GIVE EVERYTHING IN THE WORLD TO SPEND AN EVENING WITH MAX ZERO?

SHIVERING WITH EXCITEMENT AND ANTICIPATION, SHE IS LED BACKSTAGE.
MAX, HERE'S THE BROAD.
OH MY GOD, HE'S... HE'S SO BEAUTIFUL.

I CAN'T BELIEVE IT... I'M SITTING ON THE SAME BED AS MAX ZERO... NO ONE'S GOING TO BELIEVE THIS...
ZZ

MORNING COMES AND MAX WAKES UP.
WHERE THE HELL AM I? WHAT CITY ARE WE IN? WHO ARE YOU?

!
THE FOLLOWING NIGHT...

SHE STANDS OUTSIDE THE CLUB WAITING FOR HER IDOL. IF SHE COULD ONLY CATCH HIS EYE FOR A SPLIT SECOND, SHE WOULD BE HAPPY FOR THE REST OF HER LIFE.
TONIGHT: MAX ZERO IN CONCERT
HEY YOU! MAX ZERO WANTS FEMALE COMPANY FOR THE NIGHT! INTERESTED?
ROAD CREW
J. SACCO 11-93

ROCK 'n' ROLL ROT
by Joe Sacco ©1993
They're young, they're enthusiastic, and they've just formed a band...
WE JUST WANT TO SPREAD JOY THROUGH OUR MUSIC...

Several double-platinum albums later...
I'M SICK OF PLAYING YOUR STUPID SONGS! I WANT TO PLAY MY STUPID SONGS!
WELL PLAY 'EM FOR MY LAWYER! I QUIT!

Not so fast! After years of litigation, the band reforms to pay the costs of years of litigation...
MY CLIENT WOULD LIKE TO ADVISE YOUR CLIENT THAT HE NEEDS TO CHANGE A GUITAR STRING...
MY CLIENT AGREES, WITH THESE QUALIFICATIONS...
10.93

Indispensable to a well oiled music-industry machine is the...

RECORD LABEL executive

by Joe Sacco ©1994

WHEN I SIGNED THESE SLOBS, THEY WERE LIVING IN A RAT-INFESTED DUMP WITHOUT HEAT OR WATER! IT WAS HORRIBLE! SHAMEFUL!
NOW LOOK AT THEM!
OKAY, NOTHING HAS CHANGED! WHAT OF IT? WHO ARE YOU ANYWAY? I WANT TO SPEAK TO MY LAWYER!
TIBET

I DON'T GET IT. OUR C.D. IS SELLING WELL... SO HOW COME WE'RE STILL LIVING LIKE PIGS?
HOW MANY TIMES DO I HAVE TO EXPLAIN IT TO YOU?
ONCE.
AHH... LET ME GET MY ACCOUNTANT.
HAWAII

...SO, AS YOU CAN SEE, WHETHER WE IMPOSE A MARXIST OR KEYNESIAN MODEL UPON THE EXISTING HEAVY METAL MARKET, THE SUPPLY-DEMAND CURVE DEMONSTRATES...
?
?
PARIS
TOAST, ANYONE?
11·93

So we leave our busy record label executive, forever concerned with the interests of his musicians...
STILL A PROBLEM WITH THE RATS, BOYS?
NAH, NOT ANYMORE...

C SIDE: ARTIFACTS

MY FRIENDS, LET'S FACE IT, I will not go down in cartoon history as one of the great illustrators of my generation. But there was a short period — my two or three years in Berlin — when I made my living as a poster artist. Yes, a living. In those days, of course, "a living" meant enough German marks to put a roof over my head and keep me in beer and bread. Anyway, the Berlin period was the "high point," as it were, of my "rock career." Two or three nights a week you would have found me at the Ecstasy or the Loft having my ears blown out by whatever American or British or Australian band was blowing through town. In those days, with my cohort Christof Ellinghaus, owner of City Slang records, I was "glamored on sight," which meant I was let into clubs for free; my face was my ticket. I thought I was such a fucking star that I seriously considered having my name legally changed to "Joe Plus One."

The following section collects the majority of my posters from back then. Thousands of each would be printed up and sent to different clubs around Germany, and the clubs would paper underpasses and walls with them. They were large, a few feet by a few feet, and designed to be read from a distance. Individual club names, show times, etc., would be stamped or written in a blank space left under each poster. But the cartooniness of my posters was soon out-of-date. The masses wanted colorful computer-generated images and the "graphic designers" took over, that bunch of no-talents.

The other illustrations are a hodge-podge of other posters — mostly from the height of Portland's "grunge" years — T-shirt designs, miscellaneous record covers, etc., that I did to make some spare money here and there. What a waste of ink.

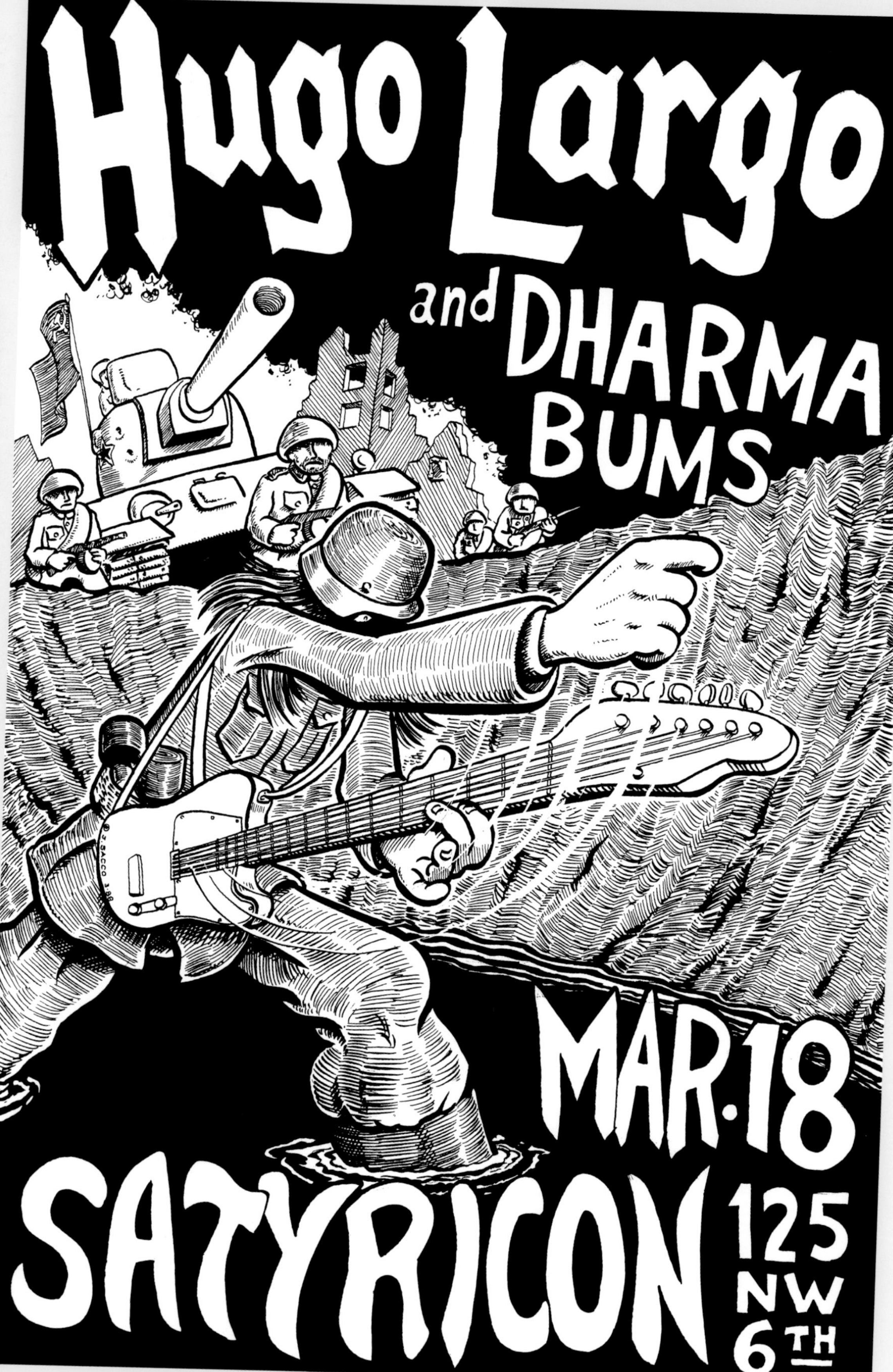

First rock poster I ever did, back in Portland, Oregon, during the Reagan administration.
I can't explain the Eastern Front imagery, but I've always had a soft spot for the T-34 tank.

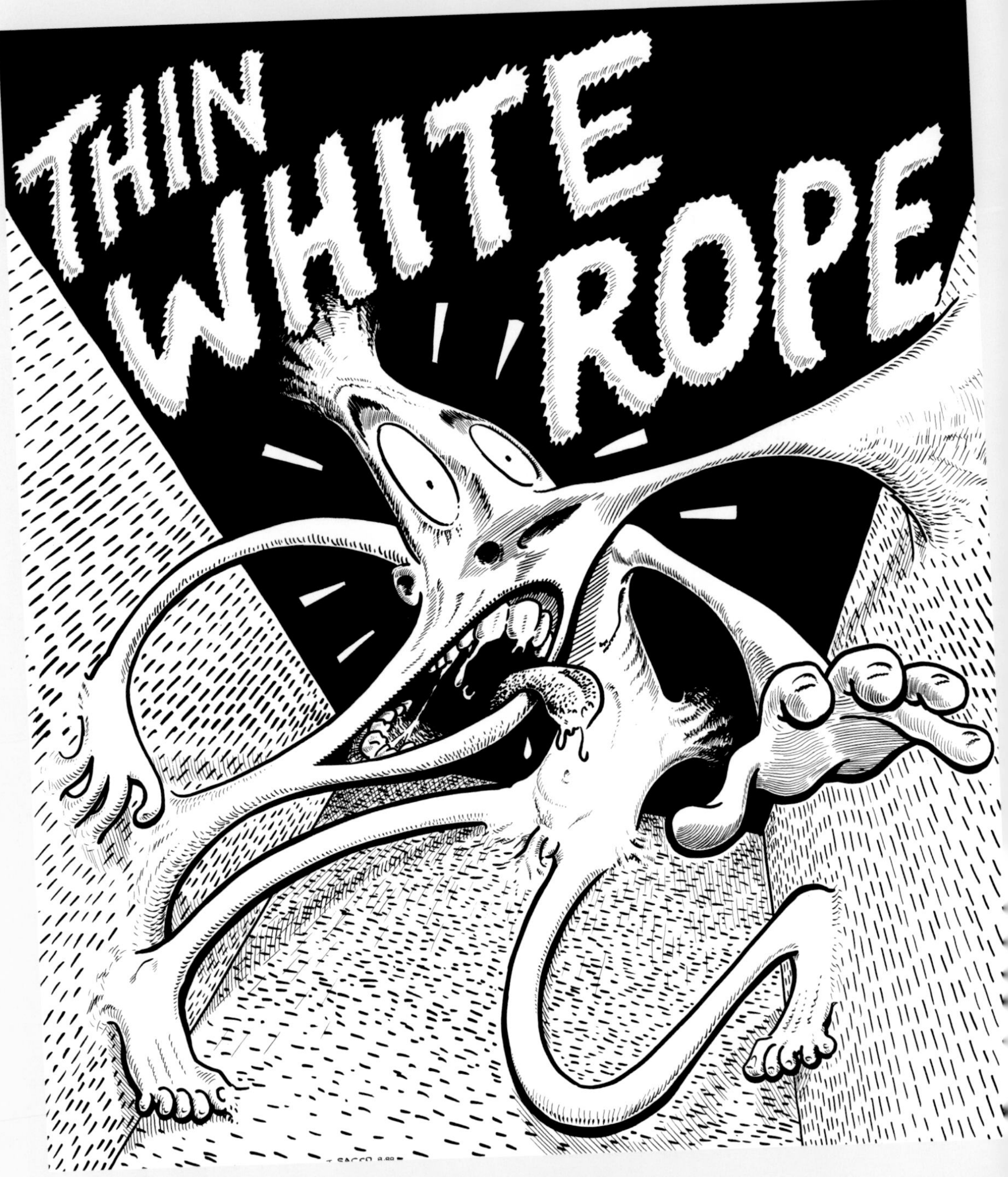

This one's from my first Berlin sojourn. I was getting about $25 for two posters in those days plus room and board. I'd draw these on the floor while Camille Lemmens and Christof Ellinghaus, who ran a tour agency called SOOMA, stepped over me to get to the fax machine.

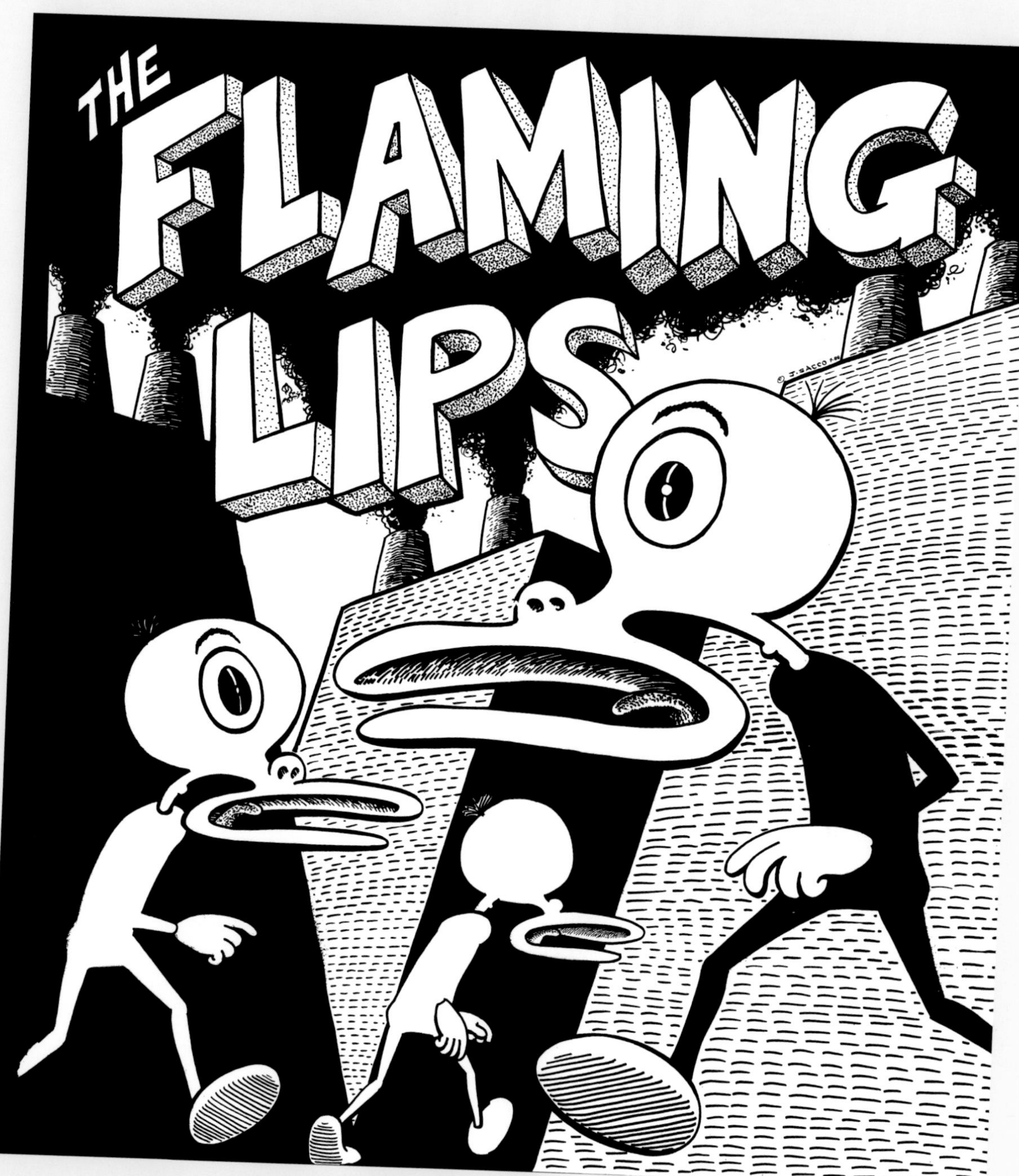

I borrowed some old characters I'd made up years before for this one, but give me a break. I was just starting out on this poster thing, still finding my "voice."

This poster was actually meant for Redd Kross, but Redd Kross cancelled so some artless German slapped on the lousy, undersized Mudhoney lettering and used it for that band instead. Mudhoney hated this poster, saying it was sexist. These are the same guys who named their band after a Russ Meyer movie, for Christ's sake. But they had some *American* girl on tour with them telling them what to think, I remember.

I used the same Bosch-like imagery for one of Napalm Beach's record covers, but my only example of that was nicked a long time ago.

I've lost a lot of original art in my day. Imagine my horror when I stepped into the offices of the Paperclip tour agency in Nijmegan, The Netherlands, and found the original of this one on someone's office wall! I was so struck by the audacity of the thief that I didn't insist the art be returned!

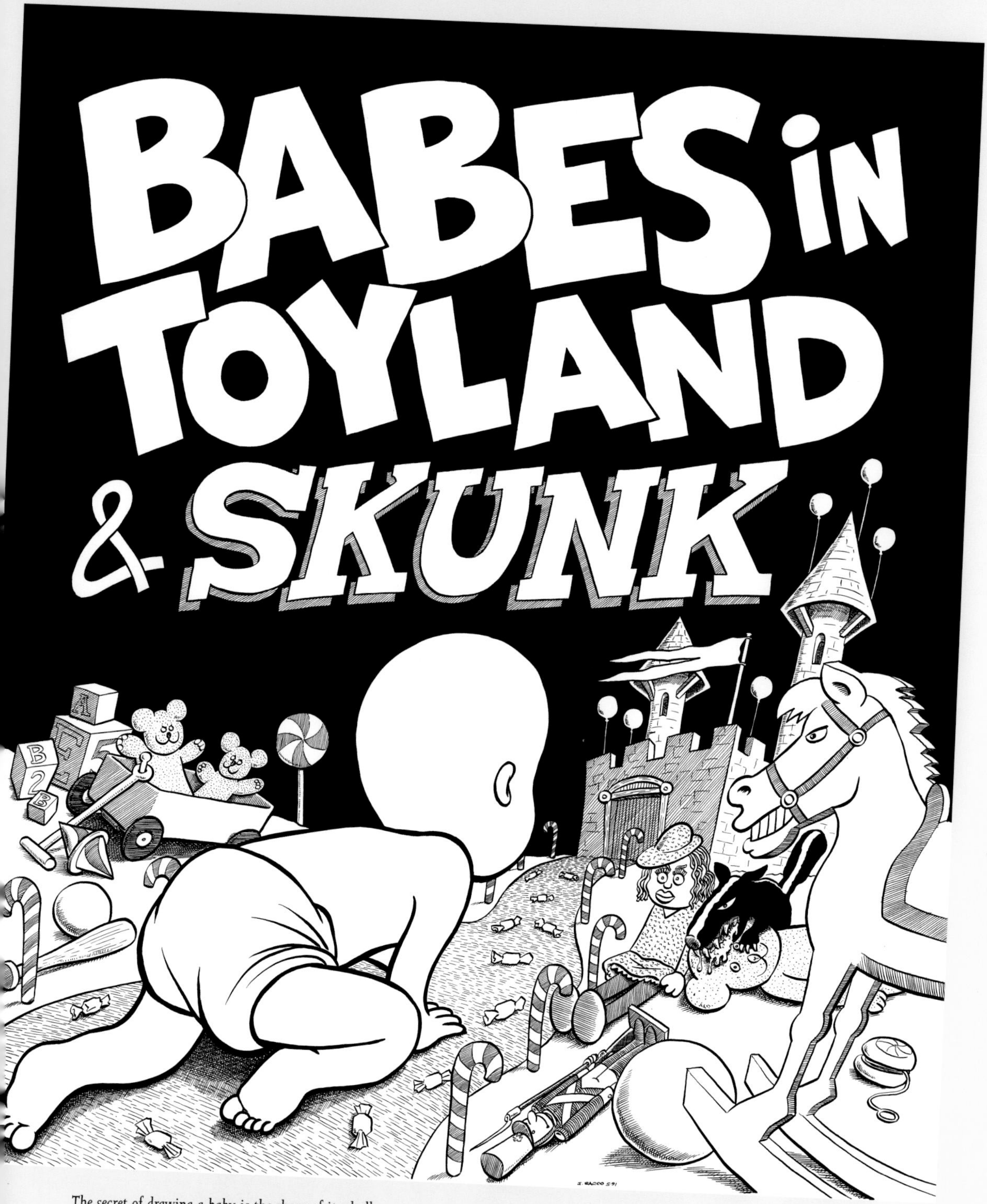

BABES IN TOYLAND & SKUNK

The secret of drawing a baby is the shape of its skull.

This poster was used for only two *Austrian* shows, and some Central European imbecile printed the blacks as purples, and the result wasn't fit for toilet paper. This image is scanned from the original.

Thin White Rope was managed by the incomparable Mel Compton, who once told me how he skipped out on a chance to meet ex-Beatle Ringo Starr. "I've got no time for Ringo," he said.

Dual bills present a tricky problem for the poster artist. I strained hard to make the image play on both band names and was rewarded with the expected dreadful result.

SPRINKLER

What can you do when one of your best friends asks you for a T-shirt design for his band? You drop what you're doing and for 50 bucks you knock out a work of genius. Then the band breaks up before the T-shirt goes into production. Sheesh.

H.P. Zinker was an *Austrian* band. I usually chain-listened to a band's albums while drawing their posters so I credit the Zinkers with those disgusting noodle things.

This one's a bit of a mess because I tried to incorporate an image from each of the songs on an Eleventh Dream Day album, thus violating my own poster dogma — one central idea only!

I've got to hand it to me. I really know how to make drawing a chore. This poster was done before computers were invented. Nowadays, a "graphic designer" could churn out this effect with the click of his "mouse."

Okay, the first one was sexist! So what about this one, Mr. Mudhoney???

Another lazy effort, but Old Europe loved Americana back before the ol' USA started bombing everyone to bits.

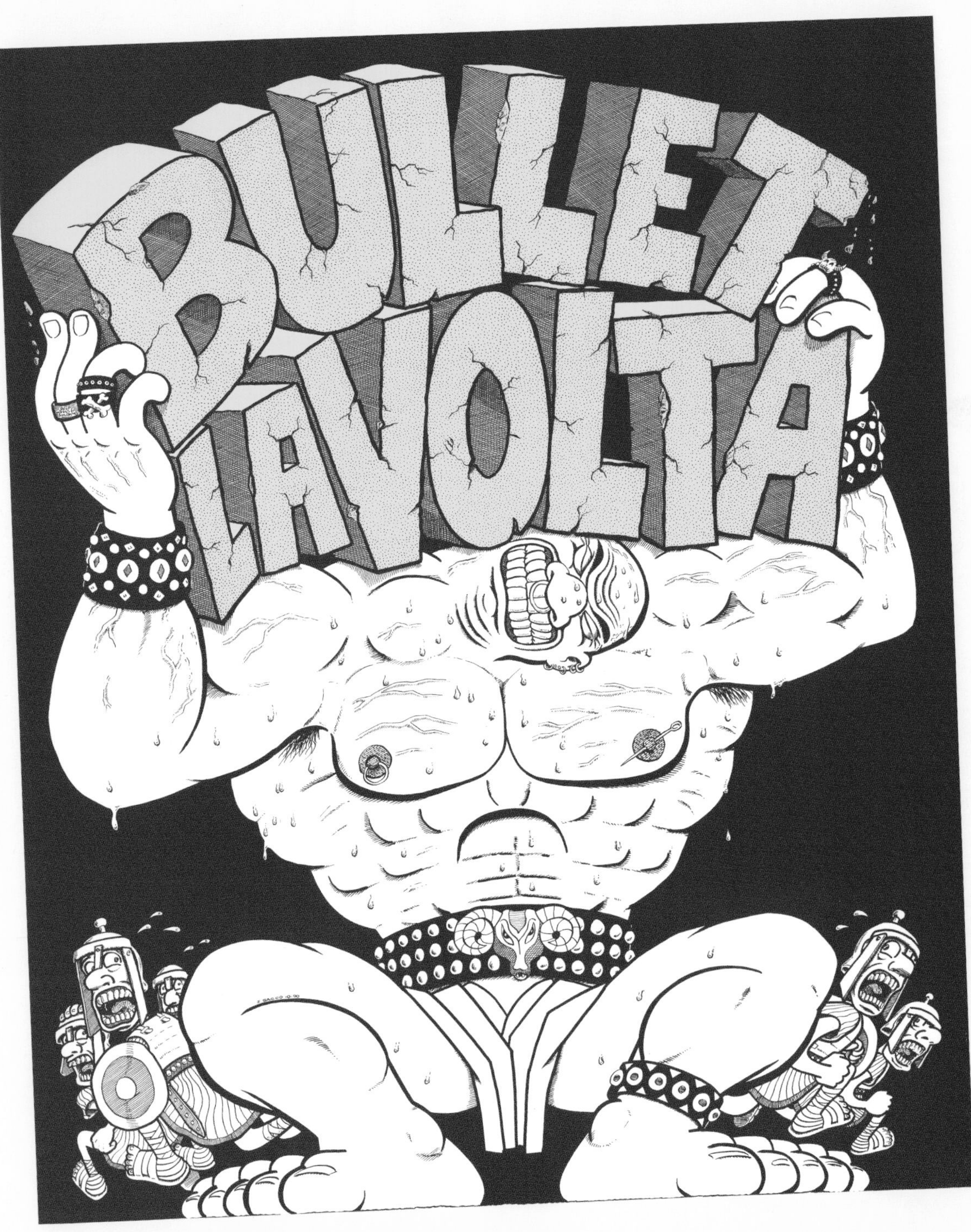

When in doubt, go for the Greco-Roman theme. The band didn't "get it," but I bet they weren't big readers of Marcus Aurelius's 'Meditations,' either.

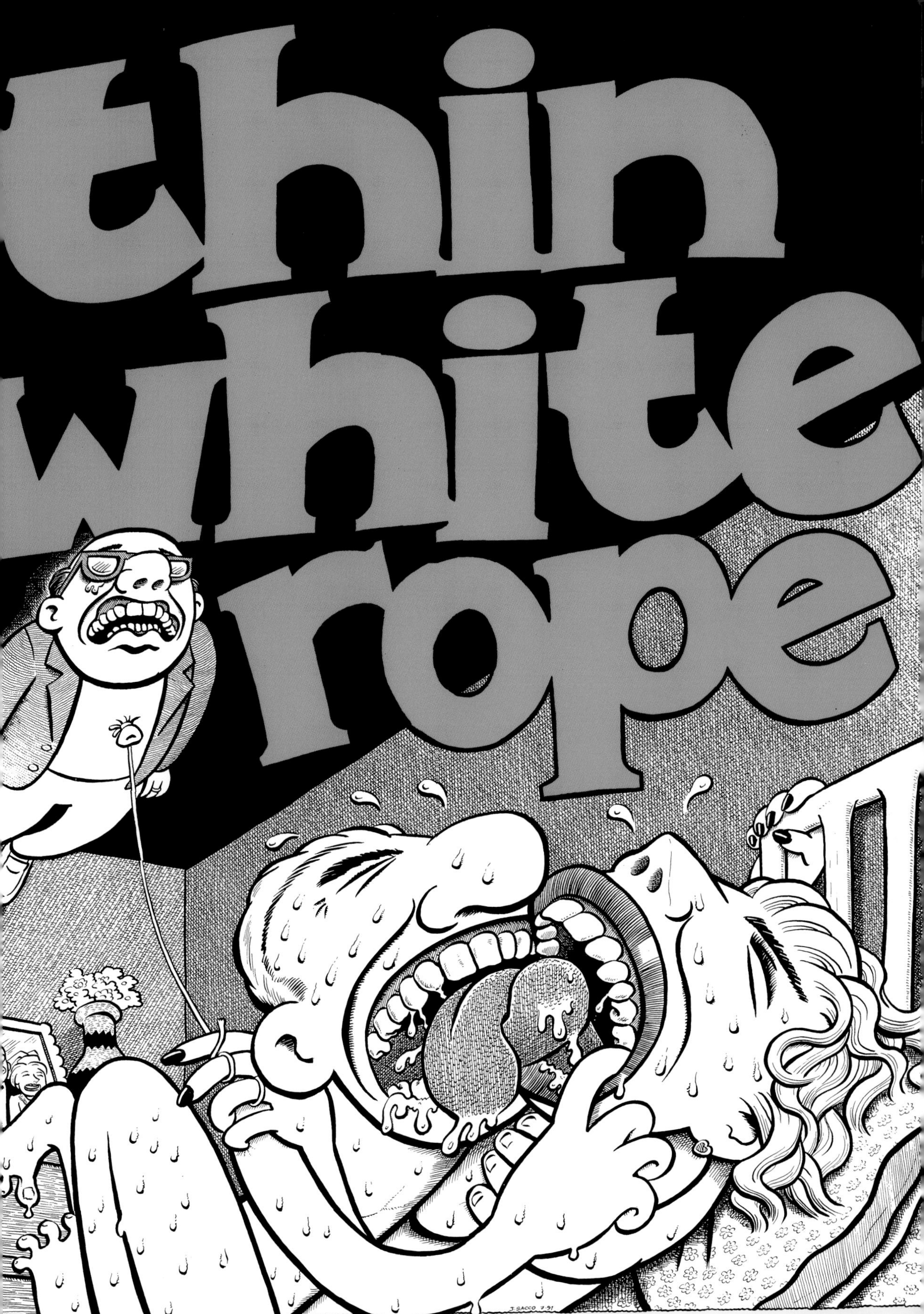

Oh dear, all I can do is apologize to Thin *White* Rope
for this bit of overly clever rubbish.

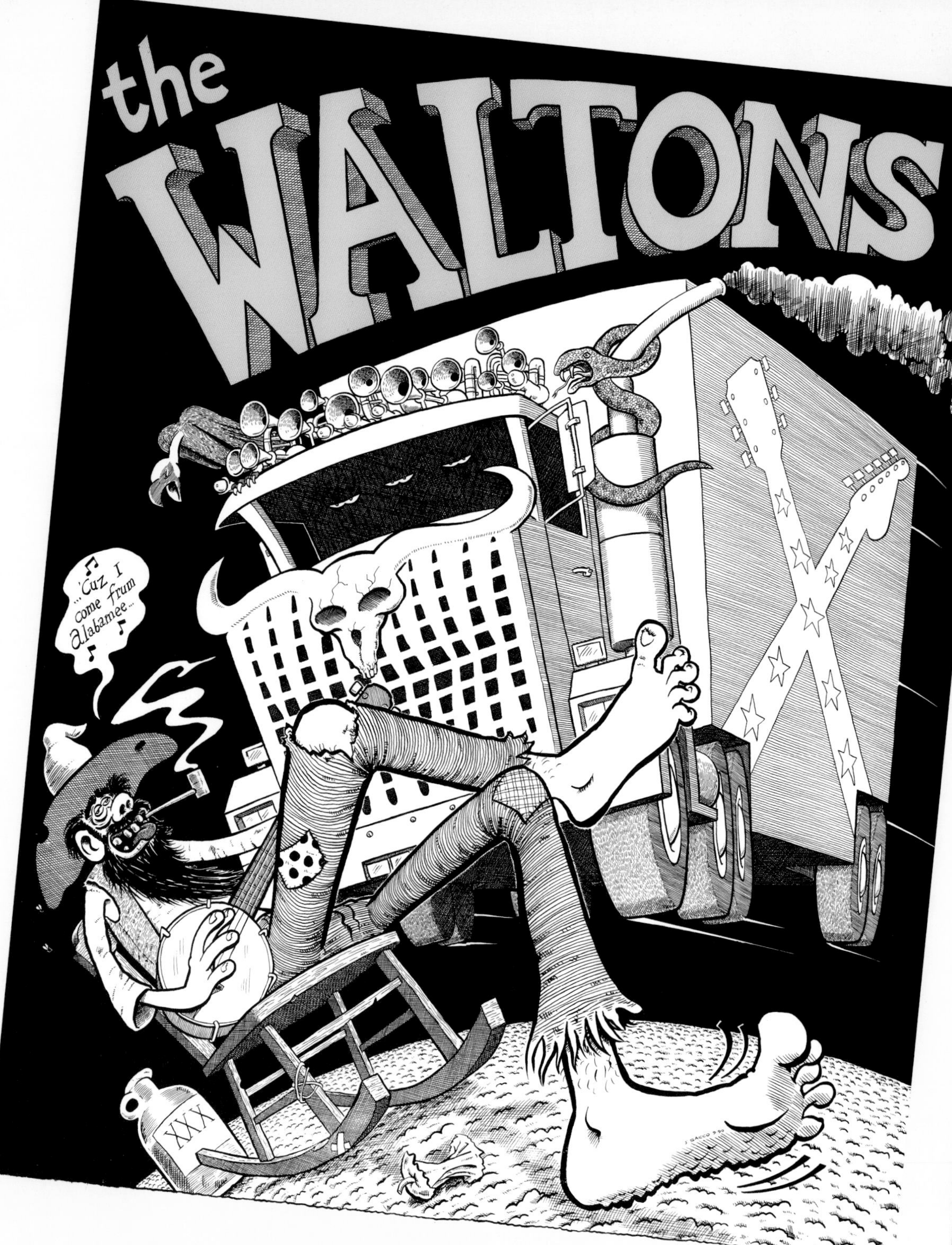

You've got to give credit to Berlin musicians who named their band The *Waltons*. They wrote shit-kicking trucker songs, and I rewarded them with this tasteless bit of South bashing.

I drew this for a biker bar. Draw a guy with a skull for a head, and you will make any biker worth his salt a happy man.

RON
COWBOY Cafe
Franken/Kyffha
Berlin
Open Satur
& Sunc
from 1p
XXX
FUCK THE MAN
J.SACCO 4-89

This was an LP cover for an awfully named record by that awfully named German band. See pp. iv–v.

This is the sort of thing I don't want my mother to see. But the band loved the cover to their double A-side single and wrote a thrasher to me called 'This is Joe.'

The big-headed figures on these two record jackets are simply painful to look at now. They make me think of those dreadful Ziggy cartoons.

BEGINN 22^{00}

AK:14

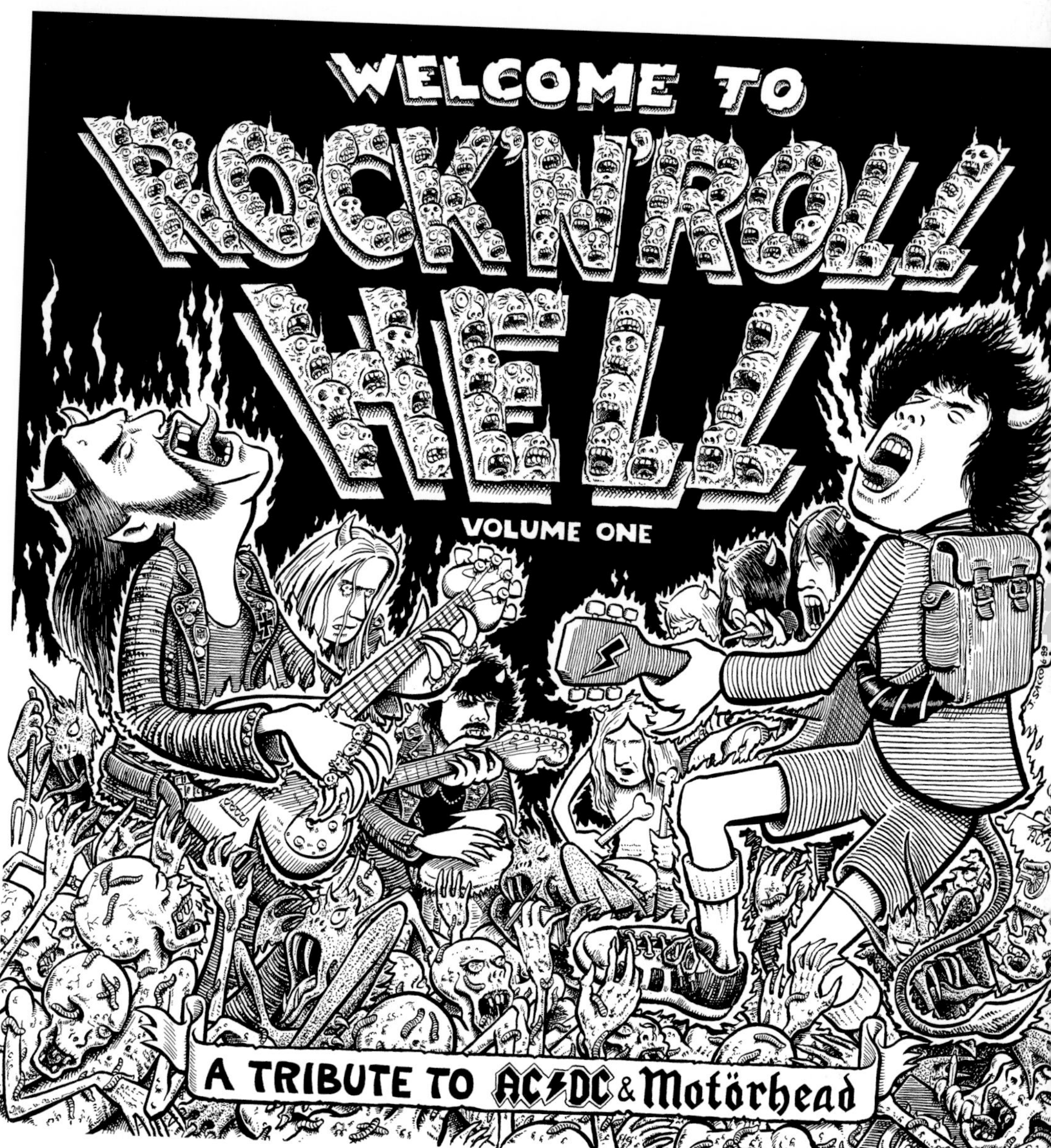

Hell was an awfully popular theme for small German record labels back in those days. I was getting paid by the demon.

This wouldn't have been a bad poster, if some cunt of a promoter hadn't decided to add the names Brian Jones and Marc Bolan in his own faux-Sacco lettering at the bottom.

I don't know what this is all about. I think I was trying to sum up the human condition on one T-shirt and gave failure a bad name.

Why Eleventh Dream Day came back to me for another design is still a mystery.

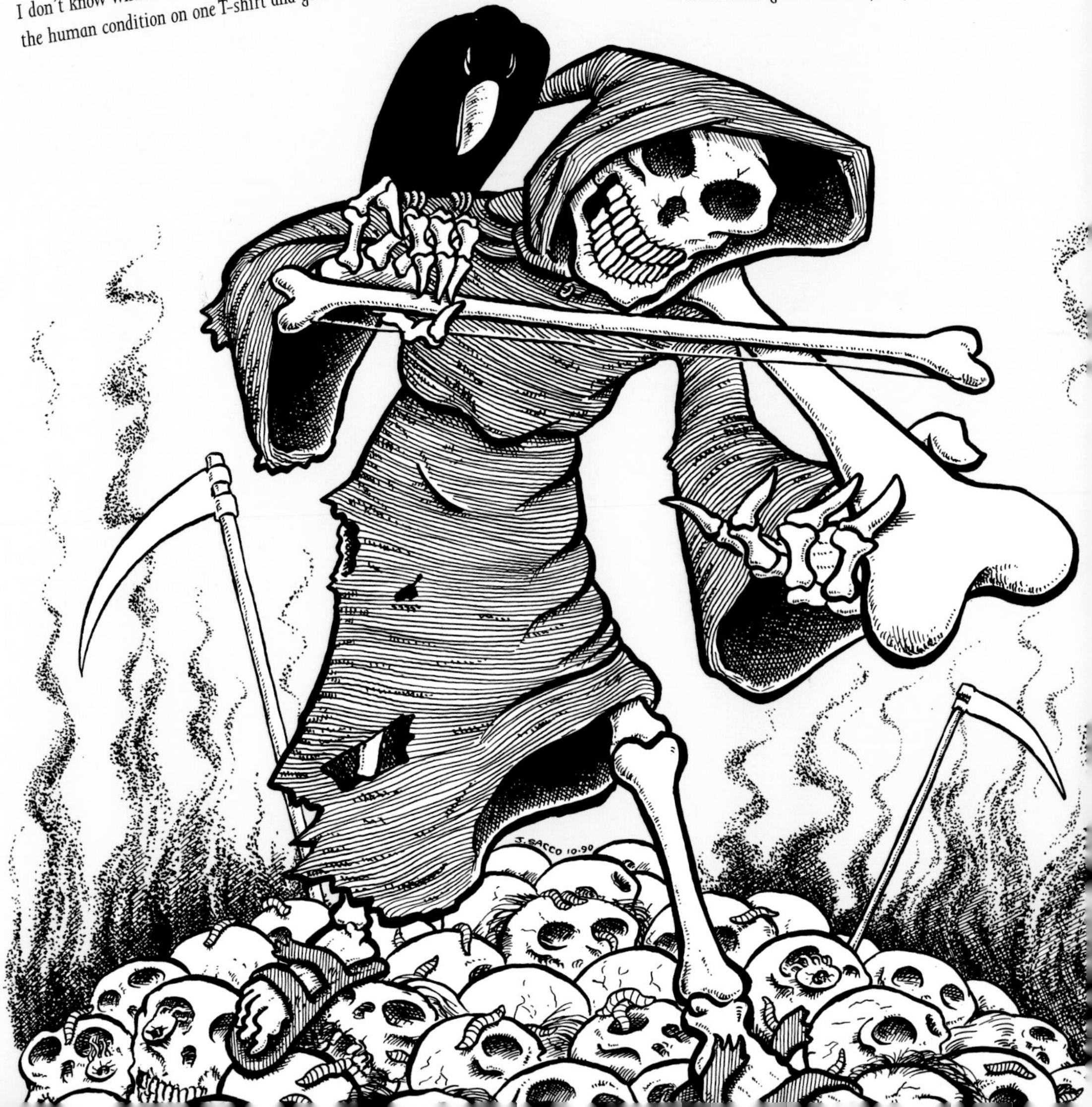

TOUR HARDER...HEAR BETTER!
J. SACCO 5.90

This illustration went with an Atlantic Records calendar. Zombies. Graveyards. Ascensions into heaven. Yawn.

This T-shirt design was meant for a Swedish doom band called Count Raven. It was never used. I drew this and then solemnly decided I would never draw another maggot coming out of an eye socket again.

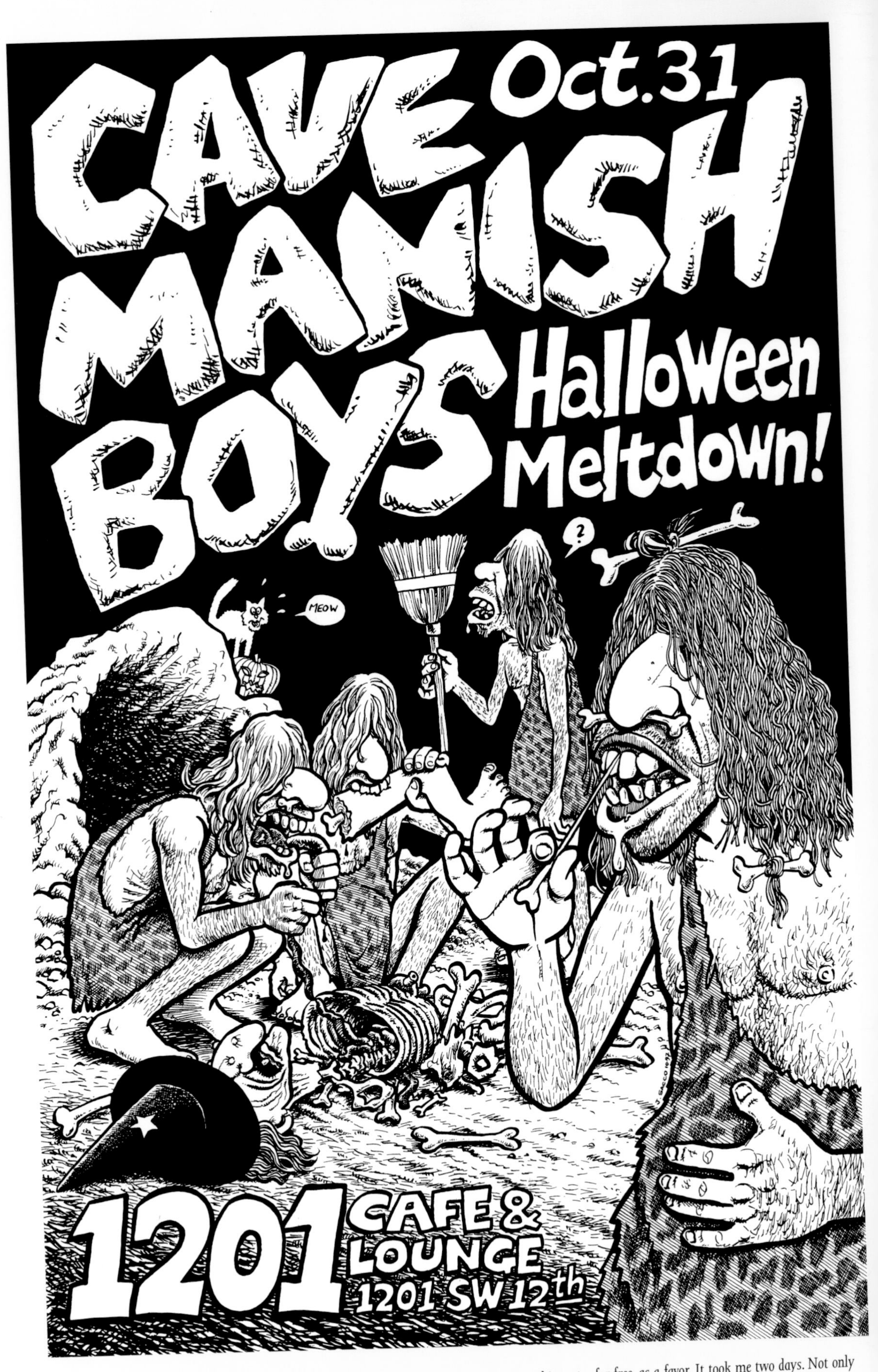

Gerry Mohr, ex-Miracle Worker, fronted The Cave Manish Boys. I drew this poster for free, as a favor. It took me two days. Not only was I NOT on the guest list, but Gerry didn't even buy me a fucking drink when I turned up at the gig. After that, I vowed never to draw anything for another rock musician ever again. And I never have.

D SIDE: NOW I'M A MAN

LADIES AND GENTLEMEN, putting this book together, sorting through old strips and posters, has forced me to revisit my inglorious youth. But what about the present? What about the future? (My present and my future, that is. We're not talking about the fate of the planet here.)

First, let me tell you that I cleaned out my record collection a few years back. I got rid of all those insipid '60s garage rock albums that I once searched so hard to find. After all, what did a bunch of pimply 19-year-olds circa 1966 have to say to me, a grown, balding man at the turn of the millennium? I am not a sentimentalist. I sold rare records at a dollar apiece as a way of saying good riddance.

I'm a different person than I was when I toured with the Miracle Workers and drew posters in Berlin. I've made a career picking over the conflicts in Bosnia, the Middle East, and the Caucasus. Let's be clear: I have a reputation now. I can't be seen thrashing around in rock clubs or talking to people with nose rings. I'm flown to universities now to talk to students. Television crews come around. I have an agent. I have an accountant. I have a girlfriend. She has a dog, for Christ's sake, whose poo I am made to pick up. And we spend a lot of time talking about mortgage payments and our knee joints. I'm respectable, y'understand? I listen to a lot of jazz now. Miles, Mingus, etc. That's right. I sip my Oregon Pinot and listen to Miles Davis. So much for the revolution, eh? So much for living fast and dying young. Let's face it, I grew up. And I'm scared I'm gonna lose it all. If I do, it's back to the barricades, you bet! It's down with the man! I'll be first to stove in the heads of the oppressors unless I'm one of them!

And that's why, as far as rock and roll goes, there's only one band that speaks to me now, that allows me to have it both ways. The Rolling Stones. Yes, you're laughing. Laugh all you want. I will write a book about the Rolling Stones when I get out of my saving-the-world phase. That's a promise. Until then I present a couple of strips about Jagger and Co. that I did some years back. "The Stones and I" and "Suffering for the Stones" were originally serialized in Portland's *Willamette Week* after appearances by the Stones in '94 and '98. They were subsequently reprinted in *Zero Zero*, the late great Fantagraphics anthology.

The blues? That's a safe bet. Everyone digs the blues though, frankly, it took me a long time to see past that noodling B.B. King stuff and appreciate the depth there. I got into the blues via the Stones. I started listening to Robert Johnson because they'd covered his songs. I liked the country blues, then the Chicago blues, then the messiest blues I could find, which got me interested in the music Fat Possum was putting out in the '90s. "The Rude Blues" is about a tour of Fat Possum artists I joined for a short time. It appeared initially in *Details* magazine. (Those gutless bastards at *Details!* They edited out the middle panel at the bottom of p. 118, which has been restored here.) Later Fat Possum commissioned me to draw the cover to a CD compilation, *Not The Same Old Blues Crap II*.

"Portrait of the Artist as an Aging Lightnin' Hopkins Enthusiast" was one of those labors of love I allow myself every now and then, but less and less frequently. This one appeared in the *Oxford American*.

ON THE OTHER HAND, MAYBE IT'S ONLY ROCK 'N' ROLL...

LADIES AND GENTLEMEN, WE ARE PLEASED TO PRESENT THIS FOUR-PART COMICS SERIES (TO BE RUN OVER FOUR CONSECUTIVE WEEKS) ON ONE ORDINARY MAN'S PERSONAL RELATIONSHIP WITH THE WORLD'S GREATEST ROCK 'N' ROLL BAND...

THE STONES AND I

PART I

by Joe "Little Queenie" Sacco ©1994

Here they come, the omnipotent, immemorial Rolling Stones, the nearest thing to religion I know... And their Voodoo Lounge tour is a mini-second coming and I've got a ticket to the rapture, Oakland Coliseum, Sec. 114, Row 23, Seat 11...

This has nothing to do with nostalgia, this is the Stones we're talking about, and they're a rock institution who've left fingerprints and smears on every decade they've touched...

In the 60's they spooked the squares with their dark, devilish ways...

In the 70's they shocked the straights with their decadence and dissipation...

In the 80's...uh...

...let's skip the 80's, shall we?

Anyway, this is the 1990's and now things should get really interesting 'cause the Stones are in their 50's, uglier than ever, and still raunchy and raising a stink... they're ignoring the naysayers and exit signs as they carve out a new niche for themselves as the world's first and foremost dirty old rock band!

I wish my contemporaries had half the juice the Stones have, but just look at 'em—20 years younger than Jagger and Co. and already goddamn wrecks! All limps and lumbagoes and layers of chin! And barely enough energy to arrange their snacks alphabetically!

Not that I'm a shining example of aging with dignity, mind you... I've been dragged kicking and screaming down the years...

I squandered my youth on education and career, and now I'm trying to make up for it in triplicate—hanging out with kids half my age, frequenting their clubs, wearing their clothes, and generally making myself a laughingstock...

The Stones, on the other hand, have aged on their own terms, and if they're not what they were in '69 or '78, so what? They're like the pyramids or some other fantastic ruin... they're cracked and toppled and beat up, but enough magnificence remains that they still take more of my breath away than most anything else that's come along since...

DEAR READER, WE ARE ON THE ROAD, FOUR PILGRIMS— CRAZY MAMA, BROWN SUGAR, LADY JANE (NOT THEIR REAL NAMES), AND I— BOUND FOR OAKLAND AND OUR APPOINTMENT WITH THE ROLLING YOU-KNOW-WHATS!

THE STONES AND I

PART II
by Joe "Wild Horses" Sacco ©1994

But before we go any further (and we have 600 miles to go), let us face unflinchingly one of the greatest philosophical questions of the latter half of the 20th Century, namely:
MOBIL
Denny's
MOTEL
TACO BELL
JIVIN' SISTAH FANNY ♫
WHICH BAND'S BETTER— THE STONES OR THE BEATLES?

It's no secret, the Beatles were my first love, and I joined their joyous celebration of all life has to offer like many a wide-eyed, well adjusted youth in his short pants.
There's nothing you can do that can't be done ♫

But the years have crashed behind me one upon another leaving a shambles of wrong choices, loves lost, and empty bags of salted peanuts from airplanes taking me to other people's cities... It's 'Exile on Main Street' and the second side of 'Tatoo You' that speak to me now more than anything the Moptops ever did...
HIS COAT IS ♫ TORN AND FRAYED, IT'S SEEN MUCH BETTER DAYS ♫

Still, I've shunted the Beatles aside guiltily, as if committing some sort of transcendent infidelity, for to embrace the Stones is to acknowledge something else is all but played out and dead in myself...
HONK
HOPE
DIED
SOMETIME IN THE 1990's

ON THE OTHER HAND, MAYBE IT'S ONLY ROCK 'N' ROLL...

That's the way Crazy Mama sees it. He's a new fan, fresh from his crash course, to whom the Stones are simply a collection of songs and a string of annotated, cross-referenced anecdotes he's prepared for the trip...
FACTOID NO. 136B: OCTOBER 1973... KEITH IS FINED £205 FOR POSSESSION OF CANNABIS, CHINESE HEROIN, MANDRAX...

To Lady Jane, the Stones are high show biz... He's hoping the concert will be a spectacle of fireworks, flame throwers, naked Brazilians, and anything else the Stones can think to pile on...
I WANT ALL THE FRILLS.

We get to San Francisco where it's Stones Stones Stones on the radio. I'm beginning to panic. I've got more at stake on this trip than entertainment. I need answers, dammit, the meaning of life...
ONE WAY
I'LL ♫ COME T'YOUR EMOTIONAL RESCUE
J. SACCO 11.94

FRIENDS! ROMANS! COUNTRYMEN! WE ARE IN THE OAKLAND COLISEUM, WAITING! THE PLACE IS FILLING UP! A CAPACITY CROWD! THE BIG MOMENT HAS COME!

THE STONES AND I

PART III

Wait! There he is on the giant screen! It's Jagger! He runs down one ramp and across stage! He runs up the other ramp! Then back to the stage! And up a ramp! And down! And up it again!

What a performance! The 100-yard dash! A four-minute mile! The 200-meter high jump! With triple axel! And now he's running a relay! He's got a baton in his hand!

Wait! It's a microphone! 'Cause Jagger isn't just a fitness video! He's a singer, too! He's clobbering us with greatest hits! 'Honky Tonk'! 'Sympathy'! 'Tumbling'!

J SACCO 11-94

THE CONCERT IS OVER AND MY MATES AND I HAVE ENSCONCED OURSELVES IN A DARK NORTH BEACH BAR TO BEGIN WHAT WILL DOUBTLESSLY BECOME WEEKS, IF NOT YEARS, OF REFLECTION...

THE STONES AND I

PART IV

by Joe "You Can't Always Get What You Want" Sacco © 1994

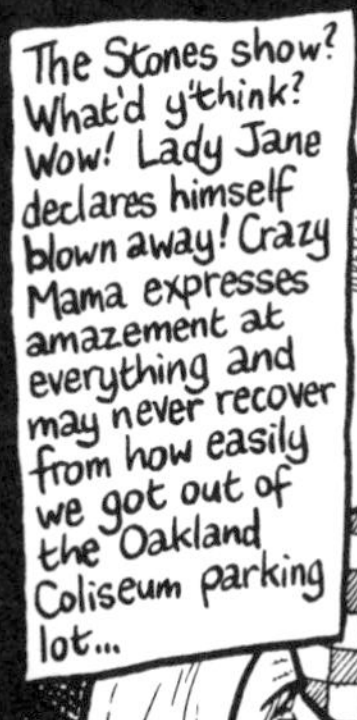

The Stones show? What'd y'think? Wow! Lady Jane declares himself blown away! Crazy Mama expresses amazement at everything and may never recover from how easily we got out of the Oakland Coliseum parking lot...

WE JUST...
THE TRAFFIC, IT WAS...
WE JUST DROVE RIGHT OUT OF THERE...
Brown Sugar, normally a man of few words and steadfast sobriety, recalls how he found himself—to his own surprise—transformed into a dancing-in-place machine...
MY EARLY MISGIVINGS ABOUT THE STADIUM SETTING GAVE WAY TO A FEELING OF ONENESS WITH THE CROWD, AND, INDEED, I SHOOK MY BOTTOM...

But I'm somewhat reticent and a little sulky... I didn't have my tête-à-tête with the Rolling Stones... I mean, it was hard to tell whether Mick Jagger liked me personally... Okay, he asked how I was doing, if I was having a good time...

ARE YA HAVIN' A GOOD TIME, A-YEAH?

YEAH!

But he was asking everyone else there, too, in multiples of 50,000...

I suppose the Rolling Stones have mattered so much to me on a personal level that I couldn't quite swallow sharing them with a bunch of mere "ticket holders"—people who probably knew the Stones only through who-knows-what shoddy "hits" repackagings and responded best to the most recognizable riffs...

WHAT'S YOUR FAVORITE STONES SONG?
FAVORITE?
HOW COMMON.

Yet those were precisely the sort of people the show catered to... To have been seduced by the Stones under such circumstances would have been to cheapen myself in their (i.e., the Stones') eyes...

AND I'M NOT THAT SORT OF BOY...

You're asking, what'd you want for your $50 ticket? Love? And to be fair, the Stones performed their set superbly, and for several moments I almost forgot that I am one of their truest disciples and actually enjoyed myself...

...I-I-I AM THE WORST KINDA GUY FOR YOU TO BE AROUND...

But as far as my relationship with the Rolling Stones goes, the concert was all but incidental. The Stones and I have come too far together for such things to come between us... I'll just have to learn to let them have their other lovers, their silly stadium flings... I know that at home, on the privacy of my own sound system, they are mine and mine alone...

I'M A KING BEE BUZZIN' 'ROUND YO' HIVE...
OH, MICK! STOP THAT!

WE BESEECH YOU TO TAKE A MOMENT OUT OF YOUR BUSY DAY TO SHED A TEAR IN HONOR OF ONE MAN'S...

Suffering for the Stones

PART I of II

by Joe "Soul Survivor" Sacco ©1998

Dear readers, what does this look like to you? Some miserable wretch, perhaps, on his way to buy a loaf of bread during the notorious German hyperinflation of 1922? No, I'm afraid it's far more poignant than that. It's yours truly about to fork over his life savings to the British pop act, the Rolling Stones!

UH, MICK?
WHERE DO YOU WANT THIS?

And what choice did I have? The Rolling Stones are the Holy Band of Obligation, and they were coming to my hometown. Reverently I presented my unworthy offerings in exchange for Rose Garden tickets, but—

STOP!
THOU SHALL SIGN UP WITH SPRINT!
LIKE, THE PHONE COMPANY?
YOU GOT IT, BABY!
M.C.I. USERS

Who was I to question the Job-like trial the Stones had imposed upon me and my fellow believers for the glory of fainting at first sight of Charlie Watts and screaming at Mister Jagger's 55-year-old carcass?

So dutifully we dialed a toll-free number (for hours) and waited on hold with our credit cards handy (while our lives slipped away) in order to wed ourselves to the long-distance carrier that promised first crack at the finest seats...

THE STONES ARE MYSTERIOUS AND INSCRUTABLE—
—BUT THEY KNOW WHAT'S BEST FOR US.
SPRINT MUST BE THE MOST ROCKING OF ALL PHONE COMPANIES.
I THINK I'M GETTIN' THROUGH... NO, WAIT... I'M ON HOLD AGAIN!
BOOK OF CHABLIS
BORN TO SPEED-DIAL

Of course, suffering is no stranger to the Stones faithful. For years we have persevered under the jeers of that insolent younger crowd who, in happier times, would have been shipped off to places like Vietnam.

THEY'RE SOOOOOOO OLD, DUDE!
THE ONLY THING ROLLING IS THEIR WHEEL-CHAIRS!
S.W.A.Y.
Blinded by OYSTERS
FORGIVE THEM, KEITH, THEY KNOW NOT WHAT THEY DO.

The Stones themselves have pushed us to the breaking point, cleverly releasing appalling product on occasion to see who amongst us would crumble and forsake them.

Not me!
WHEN I FIRST HEARD 'DIRTY WORK' I THOUGHT IT WAS THE WORST RECORD RELEASED BY ANY BAND EVER.
DO THE HARLEM SHUFFLE...
BUT AFTER A COUPLE HUNDRED LISTENS, I'M JUST NOT SURE ANY MORE.
ROLLING STONES
CHERRY RED

J. SACCO 2.98

Would our steadfast faith be rewarded by the Stones at their first Portland gig in 32 years? In the hours before the show we completed the rites of preparation much as we imagined the Stones would—bathing in cigarette smoke, anointing ourselves in wine, and keeping the company of beautiful women...

The moment had come. It was time to head for the concert...

—CONTINUED—

OUR STORY THUSFAR:
THE ROLLING STONES!
TAXI
AND STEP ON IT
WE WERE ON OUR WAY TO THE MOTHER OF ALL CONCERTS...
Suffering for the Stones
PART II of II
by Joe "Blinded by Love" Sacco © 1998

I must admit, I had succumbed to the fantasy, promulgated by many a local "news" outlet, that "there are no bad seats in the Rose Garden," that I'd be crushed up against The World's Greatest Rock 'n' Roll Band, close enough to break security and lodge myself in Ron Wood's nose...
SECURITY
COME BACK HERE, YOU SKINNY SHIT!

Fat chance! To get any further away than we were sitting, you'd have had to carve another row in the concrete wall behind us ...
ARE WE EVEN IN MULTNOMAH COUNTY?
It seemed Sprint, which had pledged the best seats for switching to its service, had stabbed us in the back.

But let's forget about that for a moment. The real down side of any Stones show is the unsettling spectacle of other Stones fans. Y'see while the Stones have aged effortlessly, like any antiquity, the same cannot be said for their audience, which long ago descended into a state of shambles. I refer you to the Seattle show, where the panties raining down on Jagger were the size of garbage bags.
YOU MAKE A GROWN MAN CRYYYYY...

So imagine my surprise—nay, my delight—when I surveyed the Portland crowd and noted that a good half could not have embarrassed the Stones at all, and I dare say the presence of a few dozen quality specimens from the West Hills' breeding grounds was an inducement to the Stones to visit our fair city again. I mean, the Stones want and deserve beautiful people.
YOU'VE GOT SOME NICE VIEWS IN PORTLAND, A-YEAH.
In this context, Sprint's shoving a short, balding, near-sighted catastrophe like myself into the rafters was beginning to seem like a sound move, one entailing personal sacrifice, of course, but necessary nonetheless.

And the show? Well, the Stones wiped away the anguish that comes hand in glove with belief and brought real redemption to this long-suffering devotee.
I JUST WANNA MAKE LOVE TO YOU...
Y'HEAR THAT?
For the length of a 21-song set, there was almost no pain at all.
J. SACCO 2·98

But my martyrdom resumed the next day.
YOU WENT TO SEE THE STONES? WASN'T MOSES IN THAT BAND?
AND THEY JUST KEEP GETTING OLDER.
Guarded by HORSES
Application for beatification pending.
FIN

NOT the SAME OLD Blues CRAP II

I CAN'T OUT-RUN 'EM, I CAN'T WHUP THESE YOUNGSTERS. I NEED SOMETHING TO STOP THEM WITH.

Burnside Style

THE WOMEN, THEY GOT CRAZY 'BOUT ME... WHEN MY OLD LADY DONE LEFT, SH**, I JUST OPENED A DOOR AND LET 'EM COME IN.

LOOKS LIKE THINGS ARE GOING BAD AGAINST ME. EVERYBODY TALK BAD ABOUT ME. I AIN'T DID NOTHING.

R.L. BURNSIDE

T-MODEL FORD

PAUL JONES

A Fat Possum Records COMPILATION

Front and back cover of a Fat Possum Records CD anthology.

It's a loud sound that comes from the deepest South, from the land that America forgot, impoverished and violent and crack-ridden Mississippi...
WHEN YOU KILL THE CHICKEN, BABY, SAVE ME THE CHICKEN HEAD...
I'M A CHICKEN-HEAD MAN...
It churns and gurgles with a relentless rhythm, bypassing prissy, single-note flourishes and going straight to hypnotism.
THE RUDE BLUES
PART I : WHISKEY AND WOMEN
by JOE "SEEING EYE" SACCO © 2000; COLORING by RHEA PATTON
T-Model Ford finishes his set, limps into a crowd propelled to delirium by headliner R.L. Burnside...
He starts shaking as much 78-year-old booty as his one hip joint allows...
IF THE RIVER WAS WHISKEY AND I WAS A DIVING DUCK...
The kids are delighted to toy with this specimen of a mysterious far-away time, to feed him drinks, to call his bluff...
They wanna see just how wicked a genuine bluesman will be...
and a gracious T-Model — who, three years ago, I'm told, wouldn't look a white waitress in the face — fondles the proffered breasts and rubs himself against the willing asses of women half a century his junior.
J. SACCO 12.99

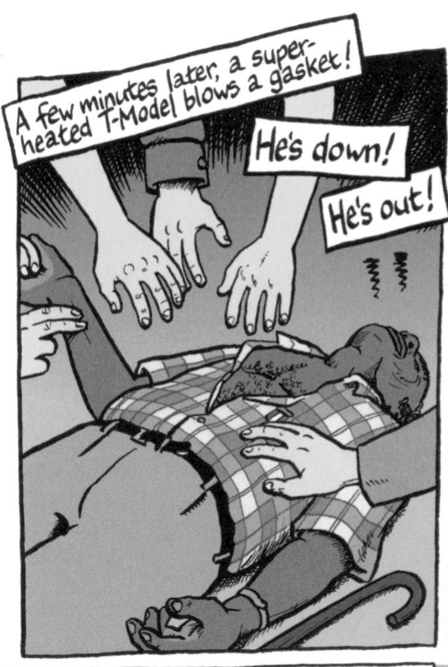

A few minutes later, a super-heated T-Model blows a gasket!
He's down!
He's out!

Is this the latest of the "last of the Mississippi bluesmen" headed for the proverbial cooling board?

HANG IN THERE LIKE A DIRTY SHIRT!

But this is a man who's been shot, stabbed, poisoned, and otherwise maimed and always come up swinging.
I'M A TAIL-DRAGGER...
I'M A HOOCHIE COOCHIE MAN...
Yes sir, looks like T-Model will live to collapse another day!
I ENJOYED MYSELF TONIGHT...
THERE ANY MORE WHISKEY?

This is Fat Possum Records' Juke Joint Caravan Tour, which has slashed through 14 cities and eviscerated any notion that the blues are a stately, genuflecting expression of the African-American experience...

PART II: THE LINEUP

R.L. Burnside. A one-time cotton picker and tractor driver... he'd shot and killed a man and done time in Parchman.

WHETHER HE DIED OR NOT WAS FOR HIM AND THE LORD TO DECIDE.

T-Model Ford. Father of 26 children... spent time on a chain gang for "cutting a man to death..."

SHIT, I CAN FIGHT NOW, BUT I AIN'T GOT BUT ONE GOOD LEG.
BUT IF I GET THAT FIRST LICK ON YO' ASS, YOU GONE!

Paul Jones. Son of a share-cropper... a welder by trade... you needn't ask why his nick-name is "Wine."

HEY! CHINAMAN! GIVE ME A CIGARETTE!

He hadn't killed anyone yet, and I was hoping he'd keep it that way.

R.L. Burnside is the big name in this bunch. He was rescued from obscurity by Jon Spencer of the Blues Explosion, who backed Burnside up on his breakout record, A Ass Pocket o' Whiskey...

SHAKE 'EM ON DOWN ...
Blues purists were aghast, but white kids pricked up their ears and made a subsequent release of ballsy remixes, Come On In, a minor smash.

And that was none too soon for Oxford, Mississippi-based Fat Possum Records, founded by Matthew Johnson with a student loan.
He ordered the most expensive thing on the menu (I was buying) and told me—
I'M NOTHING BUT A BIG DEBT HOLE.
Fat Possum, which one year logged $12,000 in check-bouncing fees and still owes one million dollars, is seemingly on a suicide mission to record the hardest, nastiest bluesmen before that species goes extinct.

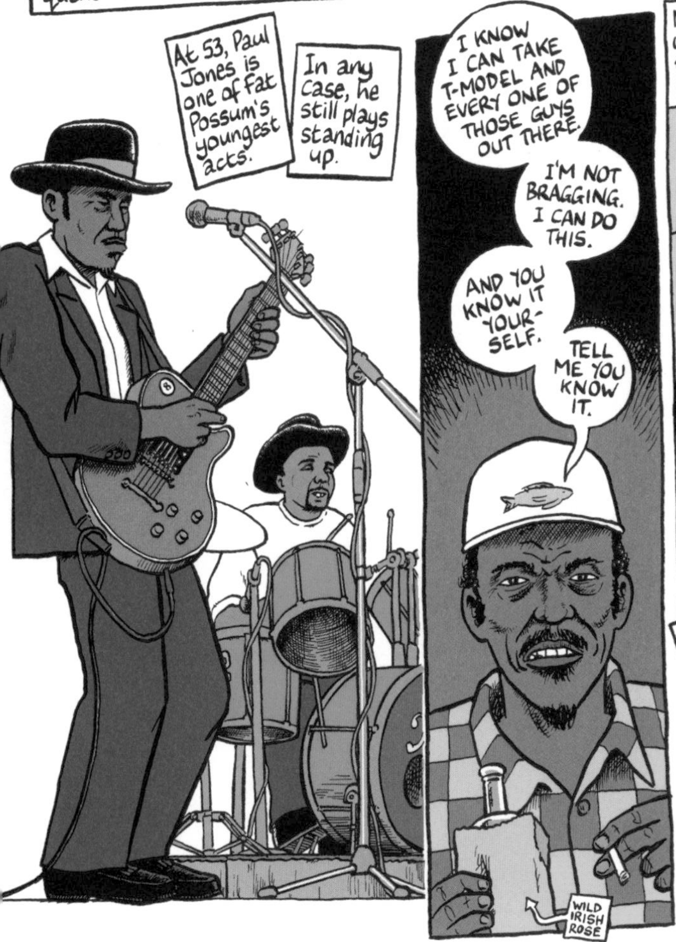
At 53, Paul Jones is one of Fat Possum's youngest acts.
In any case, he still plays standing up.
I KNOW I CAN TAKE T-MODEL AND EVERY ONE OF THOSE GUYS OUT THERE.
I'M NOT BRAGGING. I CAN DO THIS.
AND YOU KNOW IT YOURSELF.
TELL ME YOU KNOW IT.
WILD IRISH ROSE

Meanwhile, T-Model, who didn't pick up a guitar until age 58, the day his fifth wife left him, threatens to quit at one gig 'cause he thinks Paul Jones has gone over his allotted time.
I CAN'T READ AND I CAN'T WRITE, BUT I CAN COUNT MONEY AND I CAN TELL TIME.
AND IF THE LITTLE HAND IS ON THE TEN AND IT GETS AROUND TO THE TEN AGAIN, THAT'S AN HOUR.

You can't fool T-Model.
I DON'T TRUST NOBODY.
NOT EVEN MYSELF.
J. SACCO 12·99

PART III : THE BIG DARK ROAD

The tour is over and I've been asked to drive T-Model and his drummer Spam back home to Mississippi...

The whole 700 miles they don't say a word to each other...

T-Model once held a knife to Spam's throat at a recording session, and I'm told Spam has brought along a blade in case T-Model messes with him again.

Let's hope this is not going to happen in my rental.

SHALL WE STOP AT DAIRY QUEEN, GUYS?

There's a big road ahead, and I figure it's a good time to ask T-Model what makes a man sing the blues...

T-Model on his childhood:
"I NEVER WENT TO SCHOOL A DAY IN MY LIFE. MY DADDY DIDN'T LET ME. HE STARTED ME TO PLOWING A MULE WHEN I GOT SIX YEARS OLD...

"HE WHUPPED ME 'TWEEN MY LEGS, SOMEWHERE AROUND 11 OR 10, AND CUT ONE OF MY LITTLE BALLS OUT...
"LAST WHUPPING HE GIVE ME, I WAS 16 YEARS OLD. I NEVER KNOW NO CHILD BEEN THROUGH WHAT I'VE BEEN THROUGH.

On his first wife:
"MY DADDY HAD HER MORE THAN I DID. I HAD A LOW DOWN DADDY. HE DIDN'T RAPE HER. SHE GIVE IT TO HIM...

On a killing:
"HE STABBED ME IN THE BACK. OUT WITH MY KNIFE, OPENED IT WITH MY TEETH. I HAD ALL MY GOOD TEETH THEN. I JUST WHIRLED AND WENT TO CUTTING...
On the chain gang:
"THEY PUT THEM BALLS ON MY LEG. I GOT A SCAR ON MY LEG RIGHT NOW. THEY HAD US TOTING 12-FOOT LOGS. I SEEN MANY A MAN COULDN'T MAKE IT..."
And on and on, for mile after mile...
MAN, I DONE BEEN THROUGH SOME SHIT.
IT AIN'T ORANGE JUICE.
Still...
I'M HAPPY WITH MY LIFE NOW.
I AIN'T GOT IT IN MY MIND TO JUMP ON NOBODY.
LIKE IF I CATCH A MAN IN MY HOUSE, I AIN'T GONNA RAISE NO HELL WITH MY GIRL-FRIEND.
SHE DON'T APPRECIATE WHAT I DO, I HIT THE ROAD
LORD, LET ME LIVE!
I'M GOING HOME AND CUT ANOTHER C.D.
J. SACCO 12·99
PART IV: DOWN IN MISSISSIPPI
"Mississippi is the worst state," says T-Model, "the baddest state I ever heard about" though it "done got better since the Civil Rights Act got in." His house was condemned and he lives in a trailer in Greenville, a town in the Mississippi Delta.
GREEN-VILLE'S ALL RIGHT.
IT'S JUST THAT YOUNG PEOPLES HERE BREAK UP ALL THE PLACES.
THE YOUNG ONES COME AND START FIGHTING AND SHOOT-ING.
AND THEY SELLING THAT DAMN DOPE.
THAT'S WHAT MAKES IT.
COCAINE.
THEM ROCKS.

Crackheads drove R.L. Burnside's guitarist and "adopted son" Kenny Brown from the northern Mississippi hill town Holly Springs to Memphis.
I COME BACK FROM TOURING, FOUND MY DOOR KICKED IN.
THEY STOLE ALL MY STUFF.
R.L. Burnside, who still lives near Holly Springs, shows off his credentials as an honorary deputy sheriff, which means he can pack a gun.
Burnside Style
I CAN'T OUTRUN 'EM, I CAN'T WHUP THESE YOUNGSTERS. I NEED SOMETHING TO STOP THEM WITH.
HONORARY DEPUTY SHERIFF
J.SACCO 12-99
As we drove around town running errands with Alice, his wife of 50 years, this former field hand, who used to make a dollar and a half a day, told me—
IT TOOK SO LONG TO GET UP THERE, AND NOW I'M BLESSED A LITTLE BIT.
At 72 his income has reached six figures, but you'd never know it to visit him.
He spreads his wealth among numerous relatives for whom times haven't been so good.
I had a day or two to kick around before I left Mississippi, and I drove through small towns and down back roads that probably haven't changed much since Robert Johnson sang about "blues falling down like hail."
His Mississippi was violent and poor.
This Mississippi is violent and poor.
Whether or not the blues die, out here there's always been a need to sing them.
AFTER WE GONE, IF THE WORLD'S STILL STANDING, SOMEBODY'S GOT TO PLAY THE BLUES.
Burnside Style

PORTRAIT of the ARTIST as an AGING LiGHTNiN' HOPKiNS ENTHUSIAST

by Joe Sacco ©2005

What is an artist's public self but a front, a collection of personal dogmas — brand of whisky, brand of politics, brand of god — perhaps no longer believed in but argued forcefully for the sake of consistency and the benefit of future biographers.
CH
I'M GLAD YOU ASKED THAT QUESTION...

But who is the artist when he closes the door behind him? He's not so full of bluster then, when he's left alone to contemplate his diminishing creative powers and to brood jealously about his medal-bedecked peers.
THEY'RE ALL JUST AS PHONY AS I AM.

Where has the artist to turn but his extensive collection of blues?

And just what will do on a night like this? (And lately there have been many nights like this.)

YA GOTTA SAVE ME AGAIN, LIGHTNIN'!

Yes yes, ol' Lightnin' Hopkins, who wouldn't play unless he got paid up front, who skipped town to avoid taking care of his sister's funeral, whose own poor mother claimed "never has been no help to nobody..."

What does that stuff matter against any one of his brilliant lines?

SHE WALK JUST LIKE SHE GOT OIL WELLS IN HER BACKYARD

HEH HEH! THEY'RE ALL A BUNCH OF BITCHES.

The function of the bluesman, after all, is not to live an upstanding life nor to serve as a "role model" for the ubiquitous children...

J. SACCO 6.05

His function is to help the listener wallow in his own bitterness and self-pity.
YEAH, WHEN TROUBLE GO WALKIN' OUT, YOU KNOW, BAD LUCK COME WALKIN' IN
IF IT AIN'T ONE THING, IT'S ANOTHER.

And though bitterness and self-pity are the purview of any worthwhile bluesman, perhaps only John Lee Hooker, whose discography is at least as tangled and extensive, ever rivaled Lightnin's ability to ceaselessly plumb the depths of human loneliness.

So what if Lightnin' did it over and over, so what if he once cut three albums in a single week, so what if he gave it away like candy to fawning, white, coffeehouse crowds?

The artist puts such considerations aside, losing himself in his own work.
Lightnin's words no longer register.
There is just an all-knowing moan accented by aching guitar flourishes—a sound bigger than Lightnin' Hopkins the man—to carry the artist through the night.

It's late, and finally the artist puts down his pen. He's pleased with the evening's work.

PERHAPS I'M NOT SUCH A FRAUD AFTER ALL.
PERHAPS I AM THE GENIUS THEY SAY I AM.

SAME TIME SAME PLACE TOMORROW NIGHT, LIGHTNIN'?

J. SACCO 6.05